MY ANALYST'S UNDERWEAR

MY ANALYST'S UNDERWEAR

A MEMOIR

Julie Brown

Copyright © 2020 by Julie Brown

Book design and production: Columbus Publishing Lab
www.ColumbusPublishingLab.com

All rights reserved. This book, or parts thereof,
may not be reproduced in any form without permission.

LCCN: 2019906414

Paperback ISBN: 978-1-63337-281-8
E-book ISBN: 978-1-63337-282-5

Printed in the United States of America

1 3 5 7 9 10 8 6 4 2

CONTENTS

Introduction	7
Chapter One	13
Chapter Two	20
Chapter Three	23
Chapter Four	28
Chapter Five	34
Chapter Six	39
Chapter Seven	46
Chapter Eight	51
Chapter Nine	57
Chapter Ten	62
Chapter Eleven	66
Chapter Twelve	70
Chapter Thirteen	75
Chapter Fourteen	78
Chapter Fifteen	83
Chapter Sixteen	88
Chapter Seventeen	95
Chapter Eighteen	104
Chapter Nineteen	109
Chapter Twenty	112
Chapter Twenty-One	118
Addendum	121
Acknowledgments	125

INTRODUCTION

I RECENTLY READ A STATISTIC that said people who suffer from a mental illness die twenty-five years earlier than their peers. I was told by a psychiatrist at Twin Valley Behavioral Healthcare (the state hospital in Columbus, Ohio) that as a person gets older and they have more manic episodes, brain damage can occur. Sometimes I think I am writing this memoir at fifty-six because I fear my time is short.

My name is Julie Brown. I am the middle child of five. I was raised Roman Catholic in an upper-middle-class home. I have been hospitalized fifteen times. I have been in some form of therapy for various psychiatric reasons since 1984. Many of the hospitalizations were for suicidal depression, alcoholism, and mania. Medication, physical restraints, chemical restraints, psychoanalysis and psychotherapy were the methods of treatment during the fifteen hospitalizations. It was not until I met my psychiatrist fifteen years ago, in 2003, that I was treated with the right medication for bipolar disorder.

My goal with this book is to describe the long and tortuous path to a correct diagnosis. I write to describe the pain and suffering experienced before getting a correct diagnosis. I write this story to comfort the thousands of parents whose children seem lost and distant because of mental illness and addiction. I wish to educate the public about the difficulties in finding a clinician who has the compassion and intelligence to find the right treatment. I was treated by many misguided professionals who made healing impossible, and it felt like a path to hell. However, I am alive, which means there are kind and loving people who know how to use medication and therapy, leading to a path of healing.

I write the way I live—straightforward and to the point. I say what is on my mind in an effort to clarify any situation at hand. I wish I could write with the beauty and clarity of poets. I do not understand much poetry, but Emily Dickinson is the exception. I am particularly fond of this poem.

There's a Certain Slant of Light
Emily Dickinson

There's a certain Slant of light,
Winter Afternoons—
That oppresses, like the Heft
Of Cathedral Tunes—

Heavenly Hurt, it gives us—
We can find no scar,

> *But internal difference—*
> *Where the Meanings, are—*
>
> *None may teach it—Any—*
> *'Tis the seal Despair—*
> *An imperial affliction*
> *Sent us of the Air—*
>
> *When it comes, the Landscape listens—*
> *Shadows—hold their breath—*
> *When it goes, 'tis like the Distance*
> *On the look of Death—*

I used to describe situations with little emotion. I lived that way before psychiatric treatment. In the movie *Cast Away* with Tom Hanks, there is very little dialogue. His actions speak of his desperation, loneliness, and the creativity needed to survive. His was an experience I could identify with.

I was in psychoanalysis five days a week at The Menninger Clinic in Topeka, Kansas, with Dr. Mary Cerney from 1989, when I was twenty-six, to 1995. Dr. Cerney was a psychologist and Franciscan nun. She was one of very few people who fulfilled both professions. She established the Menninger Clinic Grief Therapy Center. She lectured in Europe and North and South America. Her motherhouse was in Tiffin, Ohio, ninety minutes from Columbus, Ohio. My father paid cash because I was too old to continue on his insurance policy. He did not even believe in therapy, but my situation was dire, and my parents were willing to help me in any way they could. I lovingly referred to Dr. Cerney as my "Freudian Franciscan." She died of cancer before my analysis was completed. At the end of my last session with her, not knowing she had cancer, I said, "Fuck You!" I knew she was suffering, and I was angry she wasn't seeking help. It was not her fault. Her doctor missed the cancer on more than one occasion.

When I heard she'd died, February 1995, I took a bag of bagels and cream cheese to her home assuming family, friends, and peers would be there. My intention was to drop off the food and go back to work. Nervously, I rang the doorbell. A woman answered and said, "Hello."

I said, "My name is Julie Brown. Doctor Cerney was my analyst for six years, and I thought I would drop off food for your guests."

She said, "Oh, honey, how kind of you. Please come in. I am Doctor Cerney's sister, Jeannette."

I hesitated and felt it would be too intrusive to be in my analyst's home, but she prevailed. The first thing I noticed was a pile of furniture in the living room. I did not ask her why it was there, but presumed Dr. Cerney's deep love for the Menninger Center led to gathering furniture from the clinic as it began to close its doors. There was no one else in the condominium.

She said, "My brothers are not here yet. It is so nice to have company."

She told me that she, too, was a Franciscan nun and had a PhD. She had been living with Dr. Cerney for a couple of years as she became ill. I noticed how quiet and dark it was in the room. I found myself thinking that being inside Dr. Cerney's home was wrong. What if one of her peers from Menninger showed up and saw me there? I was filled with shame and fear. I felt like I had done something wrong, but my pure intention was to drop off the food. We discussed how no one knew how sick Dr. Cerney had been, and wondered at how her doctor had missed the diagnosis of cancer. Jeannette needed to talk about her sister, Mary. I almost held my ears closed. I was too bereft to hear her name.

Jeannette asked me to follow her upstairs. As I followed her up the stairs, I noticed the railing and rubbed my hand across the smoothness of it, wondering how many times Dr. Cerney had used that railing. I noticed the beige carpet and wondered if she ever vacuumed and how often. As we walked by the bathroom, I saw her toothbrush, toothpaste, a comb, and a brush. I was moving very slowly. I knew we were headed for the bedroom. I could have turned around and waited for Jeannette to come back downstairs, but fascination and fear drove me forward. The first thing I noticed was a stationary bike sitting to the right of her bed. *Dr. Cerney rode a stationary bike?* Her headboard was big, which surprised me for some reason. *Why did she have such a large headboard?*

Jeanette had placed all of Dr. Cerney's jewelry on the queen-sized bed. Most of it was costume jewelry. When I say I was barely breathing, I mean I thought I was going to faint. This was way too much of an analyst for her patient to see. Jeannette said, "If you see a piece of jewelry you would like, please take it."

I said, "I don't think I am comfortable taking a piece of her jewelry."

"Oh, honey, look at this watch. It's not expensive. I'm sure she would want you to have it."

It was a small, simple watch with a plastic band. She handed it to me. I put it in my pocket not knowing what to do with it. While I was feeling completely out of place, Jeannette walked into Dr. Cerney's closet, and then walked out holding a pair of underwear. She said, "Julie, would you like Mary's underwear?"

My Analyst's Underwear

I froze in place and my mind fractured. *Would I like Mary's used underwear?* My first thought was to run down the steps and out the door. My other thought brought me to my two aunts who were Dominican sisters, Sister Mary Helen and Sister Mary Leo. Sisters find uses for everything. They, or at least my aunts, threw very few things away. When Sister Mary Leo got a run in her stockings, she would cut that part of the stocking out. She would then take another stocking that had a run in it, saved previously, cut out the run, and then wear one on top of another as one pair. So she had two waistbands but two stockings with no runs.

"Thank you, Jeanette, but I don't need her underwear," I said.

I have absolutely no idea what happened after that. When I left, I got into my car and started sobbing. I didn't want to know about this stuff. I didn't want to know what her bedroom, kitchen, living room or bathroom looked like. *My complete, total, and only intention was to drop off food.*

As if things couldn't get any worse, when I returned to Topeka from her funeral in Tiffin, Ohio, I introduced my boyfriend to Sister Jeannette. He had a daughter who was looking for a car, and he decided to buy Dr. Cerney's Taurus. He and I would drive around Topeka doing errands in her car. I wish I was making this stuff up, but I'm not that creative.

I drove to work at the Kansas Insurance Department and told my supervisor I would not be in the office for a couple of days. Dr. Cerney's funeral was in Topeka that night. The next evening was her funeral in Tiffin, Ohio, and while I should have stopped myself from going to her motherhouse, knowing I would be inundated with more information about Dr. Cerney, I couldn't stop. There were so many questions I wanted answered that directly related to her formation as a sister and human being. She was no longer a *tabula rasa*.

Chapter One
THE BACKSTORY

MY TWO BROTHERS AND TWO SISTERS have been and still are very different from me. My older brother, Kevin, is a lawyer and is very detail oriented. Kimberlee, my older sister, is a therapist, the protector, and wonderfully kind. Jennifer, my younger sister, is an English teacher and is incredibly creative. Billy, or Will, as he calls himself now, is funny and laid back. He works for a company that provides employee assistance programs.

I define what it means to be the middle child. I am goofy, funny, and have been ill more than half my life. When I was seven years old, my parents put a hook lock on the outside of my bedroom door. Before the lock, I would creep out of my room at all hours of the night and wander around the house. The first night I realized there was a lock on the door, I cried and screamed to be let out. I fell asleep on the floor beside the door waiting for them to unlock it.

Kimberlee, Jennifer, and Will have two master's degrees each.

I have one. I sucked in school and barely remember cracking a book. I have five nieces and five nephews who are all beautiful and unique. My siblings and I attended single-gender private schools, and while my siblings were achieving academically, I achieved athletically. I am also known for finding ways to make people laugh.

I try not to make people laugh at the expense of others, but on one particular day I couldn't help myself. In the mid-seventies, we built a home on the Lake of the Four Seasons. The area is called Hide-A-Way Hills. The drive to HAH was a bit less than an hour. Almost every weekend in the summer, the seven of us, with a dog, would pile into the station wagon and head for the hills. The house was small like an A-frame. It sat up on a hill, overlooking the lake and a beautiful meadow. Mornings were glorious. I was always the first one up. I would grab my tackle box, worms, and fishing rod and run to the dock. The sun would just be coming up and there was steam above the water. Minnows would pop out of the water; I felt happy. We swam, canoed, waterskied, and explored the streams and woods. There were deer everywhere.

The order of seating in the station wagon was: Mom and Dad in the front with Will sitting in between, Kimberlee, Kevin, and Jennifer in the second row. I sat in the way back with our Old English Sheepdog that slobbered because he was always hot.

On this day, I was eating M&M's and decided to shove one up Kimberlee's nose. I balanced the red M&M perfectly on the tip of my finger and shoved it up her right nostril. I was about nine years old.

"Mom! Julie just shoved an M&M up my nose!"

"Julie, don't shove M&M's up your sister's nose," my mom said in a nonchalant way.

"Mom, Kimberlee is picking her nose really deep and it's gross!" I said.

My dad looked at me in the rearview mirror and tried to look angry, but I heard him laugh.

I don't know why, but the next story has to do with Kimberlee too. I was about eleven and I rode my banana-seat bicycle with a plastic basket attached to the handlebars. I road to a store that was like Walmart, but this store had puppies and kittens you could buy. I picked out the puppy I wanted, gave the employee twenty dollars, and rode home with my new puppy bouncing around in the basket.

When I got home, Kimberlee said, "Where did you get that dog?"

I told her, and she said that Mom and Dad were going to kill me when they returned from Europe. Kimberlee went into overdrive. She called one of her friends who said she would love to have a puppy. We took it to her, and she was thrilled. Unfortunately, the puppy had rabies and had to be put down.

There are many stories I could tell about how I became known as a troublemaker and was blamed for most things that went wrong. My zest for life and high energy could be interpreted as the beginning signs of bipolar disorder. Some of the stories are funny, some are very inappropriate. Studies are beginning to reveal a better understand of the signs and symptoms of childhood bipolar disorder. While these two stories may not bring bipolar disorder to mind, add crying until I passed out from the ages of two to three years old, too much energy for a young child to contain, and extreme insomnia. By the end of this book, it will become clear that I was suffering from bipolar disorder and ADHD at a very young age. By the age of twelve, I began showing signs of PTSD.

My father was an expert in real estate law. My mother stayed at home and took care of us. At one point there were three of us in diapers. My mother used cloth diapers because disposable diapers were too expensive. I can't even imagine how many cloth diapers she cleaned a day. She majored in home economics. She showed me a chapter in one of her books that said the wife should shower, dress up, make sure the children were quiet, and have dinner waiting when her husband comes home. Mom followed the instructions with precision.

When my parents met, my father was studying to be a lawyer and working part-time. He would come over to Mom's house, study, and fall asleep. He showed no signs of abusive behavior, but the first week they married, he beat her. In the `40s and `50s no one talked about spousal abuse. Mom told me the abuse continued for the twenty-five years they were married. He was very cautious about when and where he hit her. My siblings and I never saw bruises on her body because he hit her and kicked her on her upper thighs and upper arms. However, we did hear the ferocious fights.

One summer day, my mom told us to go outside and not come in until we were called. I hid behind a wall inside the house because I thought they would kill each other. I was about ten years old and my mom found me hiding. She said, "I told you to go outside!"

I yelled back, "I don't want anyone to get hurt!"

There were times the abuse crept into my life and the lives of my siblings. My dad took a whack at me on many occasions. I remember two occasions very clearly.

I always sat to the right of my dad at the dinner table. Without warning, he smacked my elbows off the table and said, "When will you ever learn to keep your elbows off the table?" My face practically fell into my dinner plate.

The second incident was partially my fault. Kimberlee was studying for the SAT on a Friday night, and I desperately wanted to go to a party. I made her stop studying to take a friend and me to the party. When I got home, my dad was waiting for me. He sat me in a chair in the dining room and said, "You selfish brat! Your sister is studying for an important test and you just had to go to the party?"

That's when he smacked me with his open hand. I did not look away. He said, "Avert your eyes!"

I did not avert my eyes, nor did I cry. This made him angrier and he continued to smack me. I had nasty bruises around my lips and eyes. When I got to school the next day, one of the teachers asked how I got hurt. I made something up, but I knew she did not believe me.

I know my siblings suffered from the verbal abuse that came their way. Just listening to my parents fight caused great stress in our lives. Our saving grace was school. We were safe there. Friends, teachers, and coaches provided the love and warmth we so desperately needed.

One morning, when I was about fifteen, Mom was sitting in the station wagon in our driveway with all the doors locked. She told us to meet her at the donut shop that was on our way to school. We walked there as she instructed us to do.

When we got there, a couple of elderly men sat in the shop. It smelled sugary and good inside. We sat in a corner at the counter. The stools we sat on swiveled.

When my mom got there she said, "Your father was violent last night. I have been waiting in the car for hours to talk to you kids. I hired an attorney and I am beginning the process of divorcing your father. He cannot know this or he might kill me. I have a little money and I am looking for a house to rent in Bexley."

Even though I knew things were bad, it never occurred to me that she would divorce him. None of us knew what to say. I know I was scared. I went to school in a daze. One of my coaches asked what was wrong. I told her about the impending divorce. She sat with me for an hour, helping me process some of what was happening. There was only one person in my class whose parents were divorced. It was 1977, and divorce was not as common then as it is today.

Things began to move fast after Mom told us about divorcing Dad. Jennifer, Will, and I came home from school and Mom summoned us into the living room. This living room was the formal one we never used. This created confusion and fear in me. There was an elderly man standing in the living room when we got there. He was tall, trim, and dressed in a suit.

Mom said, "This is my attorney. He and I suggest you gather as much of your clothes and shoes and whatever you think you will need and put them in the car. I have rented a house on Bexley Park Road. As soon as we are loaded up, we are going to our new home."

WHAT? I remember thinking, *So Dad is going to come home from work tonight and no one will be here?* It was at this point I realized how afraid she was. Her life was in jeopardy.

Even though I knew Mom's life was in jeopardy, I was pissed. When we got to the Bexley Park house I angrily threw my clothes out of the car and onto the grass. "Stop it!" my mom said.

"I can't believe you are doing this! You even took Shakespeare (our dog)! Dad loves Shakespeare. I want to live with him. I don't want him to be alone in that big house! It's not fair," I said.

"Pick your stuff up and put it in whatever room you like, because we are going to be living here until the divorce is final!" my mom said.

After a cooling down period, my mom told me more about Dad's behavior. It hit me hard, real hard. I knew enough about psychology to understand that he was a sociopath. It was not only the abuse inflicted on Mom and me that clued me in, but also the friends he kept—people whose behavior bordered on lawlessness. Dad had a bookie who was one of his best friends. Another of his good friends was sent to Leavenworth for dealing drugs.

At that time, I had repressed that he sexually abused me at a very young age. While hospitalized for hypomania about ten years ago, I began to remember the abuse. My therapist, Beth, and my psychiatrist, Dr. Waggoner, have slowly helped me deal with the residual results of the abuse. I mentioned PTSD earlier. Beginning to deal with the memories brought on symptoms of PTSD. I have had to recover from alcoholism on many occasions, and deal with perseveration and OCD.

Chapter Two
THE TROUBLE BEGINS

THE TROUBLE BEGAN when the five of us were transferred to single-sex schools. My two brothers were sent to the Columbus Academy, and my two sisters and I went to the Columbus School for Girls (CSG). Both schools were very expensive and exclusive. Some of the wealthiest movers and shakers in the community attended these two schools in their youth.

I transferred in sixth grade and aligned myself with the wildest group of girls in my class. I had my first taste of alcohol at age twelve and loved it immediately. Alcohol was the perfect cure for my family's dysfunction. Two weeks a month, we gathered at a friend's house and drank Little Kings beer. Those of us who were more curious would enter a darkened room in the basement where the boys were sitting in a circle. We did everything but intercourse. Kissing was my favorite part of the game. The parents were usually upstairs having their own party. When I returned from these drunken orgies, my parents were asleep. They never enforced a curfew.

    I very quickly became the class clown. On Fridays, the school held meetings after lunch where a representative from a prestigious college spoke to students interested in attending the college. On one particular Friday, a friend and I were bored and roaming the halls after lunch. I conjured up an idea. We ran to the choir room and grabbed a choir skirt. The skirt was white, cotton, and very long. We made our way to where the college meetings were held. I crawled on top of my friend's shoulders, which wasn't easy because she was tall and we were both laughing. I put the skirt over my head, and it draped down over my friend's body. The only things you could see were my upper body and her legs. I took a deep breath and knocked on the door where the Yale representative was meeting with interested students.

    "Come in."

    My friend had to reach out from under the skirt and turn the knob. She moved forward. I had to bend my head and neck to get into the room. It was a small room with about eight students, all sitting quietly listening to the representative.

    "Do you have a women's basketball team?" I said. I stood about six feet, eight inches tall.

    Before waiting for his reply, my friend started laughing and fell backward onto the floor with me on top of her. She ran to the left down the hall and I ran to the right. The bell rang and we headed to our next class. Ten minutes into Russian history, I received a note from the headmaster. It read, *Mr. Chapman would like to meet with you now.* My friend, who was in math class, received the same note. I got up out of my chair, nodded to my teacher, and walked slowly down the hall and the stairway to his office. My friend and I arrived at the same time.

She said, "What do you think he wants to talk about?"

The headmaster, Mr. Chapman, was my friend's father, and I had a pretty good idea why we were standing in front of his office. The secretary had a desk to the right of his office. She said, "You may go in. He is waiting for you two."

As we walked in, I noticed our field hockey coach sitting at the back of the office with her hand over her mouth.

"Please have a seat," the headmaster said.

We slowly walked to his huge desk and sat down.

"So, what have you two been up to?" Neither of us said anything.

"Well, the Yale representative talked to me fifteen minutes ago and was quite upset. The students who are interested in Yale are also angry. Can you imagine why?" Still, we said nothing.

"Whose idea was it to turn yourselves into a nine-foot-tall basketball player?"

I looked up and said, "Mine."

There was a very long pause. You could hear a pin drop.

He said, "That was the funniest damn prank I've ever heard of! Now get out of here and act as if you have been punished. Oh, and apologize to the girls in the room."

Relieved, we turned to leave his office and noticed the coach holding back a smile. Her eyes said everything. They were twinkling as if to say, *Well played.*

The field hockey coach was my favorite teacher. She got me interested in playing field hockey, which in turn started my love for organized sports. While my siblings were excelling academically, I began excelling in sports. In addition to field hockey, I played basketball and ran track.

Chapter Three
HIGH SCHOOL AND MY FIRST YEAR IN COLLEGE

THE HOUSE WE RENTED on Bexley Park Road was small compared to the house we used to live in as a family. There were four bedrooms, one bathroom, a small kitchen, and small dining room. The TV room was about the size of our kitchen in the family room. I loved the house and the neighborhood. The streets were made of brick and lined with huge old trees. We could walk to school. Jennifer, Will, and I spent every Sunday with my dad. We spent most of this time studying. He either took us out to dinner or cooked. My father kept a couple of cases of Cabernet Sauvignon in the pantry. I began sneaking wine up to my bedroom, and instead of studying I would get drunk. No one ever noticed.

One snowy winter night after being with my father, I was walking Shakespeare when I collapsed into a pile of snow, thinking, *I could lie here forever and maybe freeze to death*. The alcohol numbed me to the cold. I was at a low point in my life and suffering from depression.

My saving grace was our next-door neighbor. Mo and David lived one house to the east of our house in Bexley. They were a young couple with three children. I befriended David first. We jogged a couple mornings during the week before I went to school and he went to work. David and I met at 6:00 a.m. and jogged five miles through the darkened streets of Bexley. We kept up a good pace. We usually headed for Jeffrey Mansion, jogging on a dirt trail next to Alum Creek. David was the president of his investment firm, and Mo took care of the children. When David became too busy to jog in the morning, Mo and I became friends. After school and on Saturdays, I played with the kids and tagged along when Mo had errands. She knew I was struggling with alcohol, and she did her best to encourage me to talk about my family and school.

One horrible Saturday night, I got drunk and bought a handgun. I did not load it because I was too drunk to figure it out. I passed out in Mo and David's hammock. In the morning, I awoke to find their youngest son trying to climb into the hammock. The gun was lying next to me. Mo walked out and saw the gun. She quickly grabbed her son, took him inside, and came back out and got the gun. She took me home and talked to my mom. I honestly do not remember what happened after that. I know I did not go to therapy or talk to the counselor at school.

The drinking combined with self-destructive behavior might have clued people in that I was suffering depression and possibly showing signs of bipolar disorder. I could swing from depression to high energy in one day. My grades were average and I was one of the best athletes in the school, so no one noticed the changes in my mood.

My performance in athletics only got better. Field hockey, basketball, and track helped lift my spirits. There are many stories to tell about each sport, but a track meet in May of 1980 is emblazoned in my mind. The event was the 400-meter dash. Qualifying for the state tournament was at stake. I was ranked as one of the top runners, so I got the third lane. My coach knew I was so nervous that I felt like I would puke. He told me to run a mile before the event to ease the tension.

"Julie, you can win this. Stay within yourself, keep your eyes on the track ahead of you, and do your best. I know you can do this." The bleachers were filled with excited friends, family, and schoolmates. The track looked huge! The sky was deep blue, and the temperature was in the mid-seventies.

The gun went off and we sprinted forward. Halfway around the track, I merged into the second lane and quickly realized the girl in front of me and the girl to the right of me were slowing down. They were on the same team. I had two choices: get disqualified by stepping off the track to the left, or slow down and go around the two team members. In a split second I made my move. I slowed down, went around the girl on my right, passed the girls in front of me, and won handily.

I had just qualified for the state track meet held in The Ohio State University football stadium (also known as the Shoe). The crowd burst into cheers as I crossed the finish line. My brother Kevin was on summer break from Notre Dame. He and his friends were cheering the loudest. My coach ran up to me and said, "I knew you could do it, and I knew exactly what you were thinking." He continued, "All I could think was, just don't step to your left or you will be disqualified."

The state tournament was a different story. I was overwhelmed by the size of the venue and prayed I would jump the gun and be disqualified. I came in eighth out of ten. I wasn't disappointed. I was glad it was over and I would never have to run in a track meet again.

My Analyst's Underwear

I had no idea where to apply for college. I remember a conversation I had with one of my teachers about college.

She said, "Julie, it is about time to start thinking about where you want to go to college. Are you thinking about what part of the country you would like to study in, or any specific school?"

"I have no idea. I've always loved the east coast, but I don't think my grades are good enough to get in anywhere reputable."

I applied to Boston College, Tufts University in Medford, Massachusetts, and Carleton College in Minnesota. I had the application to the University of Pennsylvania, but as I read through the application, I knew I was out of my league and threw the application into the fireplace. I was accepted into Tufts and Carleton. I think the headmaster had something to do with getting me into Tufts. With my grades, there was no way I had a high enough GPA to be accepted. I decided to go to Tufts, the most expensive university in the country at that time (1980).

My father and I flew to Boston, rented a car, and drove to Medford. I was scared and did not want to leave home. I had one suitcase and a backpack. My father helped me get settled into the dorm, then turned and walked away. I looked out the window of my room and saw him pull out his handkerchief and wipe his eyes and nose. That made me cry. The room was tiny. My roommate was all moved in and she chose the lower bunk. I was surrounded by dull gray cinderblock. The floor I lived on was co-ed with shared bathrooms. The nights on our floor were loud with music and raucous behavior. Guys played football in the halls.

I suffered homesickness and depression. There were Sundays when I never left my room. I never studied and spent every afternoon training for field hockey, basketball, or lacrosse. My best friend Kate and I spent our time training, making fun of sororities, and going to fraternity parties. I stopped drinking. None of my teammates drank, and it had a positive effect on me. I dated and went to dances. In the spring of 1981, the men's and women's teams shared a Greyhound bus heading home from a lacrosse tournament.

I told Kate, "See that guy who is asleep three rows up? I'm going to ask him out on a date."

His name was Hugh and our first date was a five-mile jog. He told me later that he was terrified that he would not be able to keep up with me. He was about five feet, nine inches tall, had dark blond hair and the cutest smile. We dated until I dropped out after the end of the year. Depression and intense anxiety were weighing heavily on me. I knew my parents were battling in court about their divorce, and I wanted to come home. I felt the need to be around them even though the environment was laden with hatred. I returned home in the spring and had no idea what to do next.

Chapter Four
THE BACK COUNTRY

IN 1981, I dropped out of Tufts. I returned to Columbus and slipped into a deep depression. In some recess of my brain, I knew I needed to put off going back to college. I enrolled in a program called the National Outdoor Leadership Program, which was stationed out of Lander, Wyoming. On the application I wrote: *I need to find myself.* I was accepted into a three-month course that taught participants how to navigate and survive in the mountains, the desert, and various other terrains.

When I arrived, I was greeted by one of our guides who helped me pick out the right size backpack, better boots than I had, a coat that would withstand the cold I would be enduring as we hiked farther into the mountains, and a sleeping bag that was designed to keep me warm at below-freezing temperatures. There were eight other students who were in their late teens and from various parts of the country.

The first night in Lander, we shared a meal and attended a class on what to expect in the next month. Three guides would be with us throughout the trip. The guides, one woman and two men, instilled confidence in me. They answered many of our questions—everything from what we would eat to how heavy our packs would be. I was overwhelmed but excited and ready to begin the journey. I was immediately interested in a woman named Liz. She was my age and we shared similar interests. She was tall and had long blonde hair. We talked about feeling nervous and insecure about what we were going to begin.

The next morning, a bus took us to the trailhead. I stepped out of the bus and thought, *This can't be too hard.* The trail was flat and there was very little gradation. After four hours of hiking, we were all exhausted. Our packs weighed fifty pounds and our feet were blistered from the rubbing of our new boots. We were hot and hungry. We made camp and began preparing for dinner.

We were almost above the tree line, and as night descended the temperature dropped quickly. I slept in my clothes because that extra layer kept me that much warmer. I also knew that if I had to pee, I did not want to walk out of the tent naked.

One night, about a week into the hike, I was awakened by the sound of movement and grunting outside the tent. I lay very still. My immediate thought was that a bear had wandered into the campground and was sniffing around for food.

"Do you hear that?"

My tentmate said, "Yes. What if it's a bear? Did we put our food somewhere that the bear could not reach?"

"I don't know. I was too tired to think about that."

The snorting moved closer to our tent and then it moved farther away. I peeked out of our tent and saw nothing. The sky was filled with stars, but the moon was not visible. When we met for breakfast the next morning, one of the group leaders assured us that what we'd heard was not a bear but a moose.

We continued our trek that day, and we were drawn deeper and higher into the Wind River Mountains. By the end of the week, we reached snow-covered mountains. The view was stunning. We were surrounded by the highest mountains I had ever seen. To make it even more beautiful, there was a medium-size lake a half a mile below us. Seeing the beauty brought me as close to a spiritual experience as I had ever had. I had no thoughts about going back to school or how my parents were holding up. My depression disappeared the first day we began our long hike. We camped around the lake and stayed two days exploring the area.

We were all stinky and sweaty. We changed our socks every couple of days, but the rest of our clothes needed a break. We rinsed our clothes in the lake and laid them out on rocks to dry. I decided to take a nap, and when I awoke it was dark, my tent was gone, and there was a strong smell of smoke in the air. I could not believe what I saw. My peers and the group leaders put all of our tents together to make one very large tent. While I was sleeping, everyone gathered rocks and dead wood and piled them in a dugout pit. A fire was heating the rocks creating a sauna. Everyone took off their clothes, crouched to get into the tent, and we began scratching the back of the person in front of us. I had never been naked in front of anyone before and was self-conscious. That feeling passed quickly when I realized how much fun we were having. Dirt filled our fingernails as we scratched each other's backs. The heat generated from the rocks felt glorious. I slept like a baby that night.

Two weeks into the mountains, I began getting an eerie feeling that something was very wrong. I wasn't depressed, but I was experiencing high anxiety. I kept it to myself for one day. The next night, I told the group leaders about my anxiety. One of the leaders said, "It probably has something to do with the altitude. There is less oxygen in the air. Many people feel this. If you would feel safer, sleep with us in our tent."

I chose not to sleep in their tent. The anxiety only got worse. I did not sleep that night, and at dawn I made a decision I will never regret. The sun was not yet over the mountains. While eating breakfast I told the group of my decision.

"I have decided I have to hike out of the mountains. I can't shake my anxiety."

No one understood the danger and fear I was feeling, and they were angry. The group leaders said nothing, and my friend Liz tried to convince me to stay. Nothing anyone said could change my mind. One of the male group leaders gave me a topographic map and said, with no emotion, "I don't understand why you are doing this, but if you have to go, go. Follow the map below the tree line. You will come to an opening where you should see men with trucks. They will be gathering wild horses. They will take you back to Lander and from there you are on your own."

I had no idea how to read the topographical map. Earlier in our hike, we were taught how to read elevation and how to avoid dangerous terrain. The map wasn't exactly hard to read, but due to my nervousness or ADHD, I didn't have a clue how to follow it. No one said goodbye or wished me luck. I felt terrible that I was quitting the hike. I felt worse about leaving my friends.

I broke the circle around the camp, put on my backpack, sadly said goodbye, and did not look back. The sun was shining bright, and I hiked for the next fourteen hours. I have absolutely no recollection of the hike. I don't know if I ate, peed, or stopped to rest along the way. I couldn't figure out how the group leader knew I would be meeting up with the cowboys. They had to have some type of communication device, but I never saw them use it.

At dusk, I came over a ridge and saw the trucks and horses loaded up. Just as one of the men was about to shut the truck door, I yelled, "Wait, wait!" He heard me, and they all got out of the truck. The experience was surreal. Fourteen hours ago, I was surrounded by friends and snow-covered mountains, and now I was surrounded by men I did not know. I felt safe. They drove to a base camp and I slept in a very cold, very lonely bunkhouse. The next morning, they dropped me off in Lander, and within two days I was lying in bed in Columbus, depressed and confused by what I'd done. The anxiety was gone.

Why did I quit? Why didn't I wait for the anxiety to pass? Why did I leave my friends? What was I going to do now? All of my friends from high school were in colleges and universities throughout the country. On my application to NOLS (National Outdoor Leadership School) I wrote that I wanted to find myself, and now I was completely lost.

A week after I hiked out, Liz called me from a hospital in Wyoming. "How did you know?" she said. Then she said it again, "How did you know?"

"Liz, how did I know what?"

"The afternoon you hiked out, a snowstorm blew in. It was extremely windy, and the snow was coming down hard. We tried to hike to lower terrain, but the storm was severe so we trenched in. The leaders called for rescue helicopters, but because of the intensity of the storm, they could not land. Most of us are in the hospital with some form of frostbite. Some of us got severe frostbite on our feet, faces and hands."

    I never heard from Liz again. How did I know? I only have two ideas about what might have happened. I don't believe in God, so I immediately counted that out. When animals sense impending danger they will move to higher ground or lower ground depending on the perceived danger. It has something to do with the change in barometric pressure. Is it possible that I felt a change in the pressure that triggered my anxiety and compelled me to get to lower terrain? The other idea is that I have a highly attuned inner voice. The anxiety and fear I was feeling could have been a result of my inner voice telling me that danger was imminent and I had to leave the group. I have had this happen once since the mountain trip, and it saved my younger brother from a disastrous hike back up Tallulah Gorge. In both instances, I had no recollection of how I got people out of danger. I somehow knew that what was happening forced me to take extreme measures. Since that time, I have listened intently to my inner voice.

Chapter Five
ACUTE PSYCHOTIC BREAK FOLLOWED BY CLINICAL DEPRESSION

WHEN I RETURNED FROM WYOMING I lived with my dad. I had no idea what to do next. I could barely get out of bed. I felt incapable of working or going to school. This was my first experience with clinical depression. Clinical depression was very different from anything I felt before. I had no appetite, no energy, no desire to go out. I couldn't sleep and felt incapable of taking care of myself. Most days and nights I would lay awake in bed, obsessing about how to break free of this hell.

I talked to my dad about how I was feeling. He said, "Why don't you take a couple of classes at Capital University? It's a small school and maybe something will interest you."

I followed his advice and took three classes that I thought might be easy enough to ease my pain. A month into classes, I had my first psychotic break. I was sitting in the living room studying when, in a very quick period of time, my mood lifted and I felt high and could not stop talking. I talked to anyone who would listen. What I said did not make much sense. I told my dad that I was the second coming of Jesus, and I thought there was a stigmata forming in my right hand. As I become more and more agitated, I also became paranoid. I felt that people at Capital University were following me around to hurt me. While driving, I "knew" other drivers were following me to find out where I lived in order to harm me. I heard voices in my head that directed me to a downtown police station to tell them I knew who murdered the wife of the client of my attorney uncle. The police called my dad and he took me home. He was angry and confused.

The next day, I felt I was in imminent danger. I drove my hatchback to where my mother lived. The road to her home was treacherous and filled with twists and turns. I took my hands off the steering wheel and said, "God, if I am the second coming, I am going to take my hands off the steering wheel and let you decide if I live or die." I grabbed the steering wheel just as I was about to careen off a steep hill.

I burst into my mom's house saying, "I am the second coming of Christ. I'll prove it."

She was living in our house on the lake. I made her follow me down to the lake where I said, "I am going to step off this dock and walk on water."

"Julie! Stop this! What is happening to you? Let's go back up to the house. You are scaring me."

She convinced me not to step off the dock, and I followed her back to the house. It was nighttime and my mom was scared enough that she made me sleep with her. At midnight I yelled, "THERE ARE BUGS IN THE CEILING!" I did not mean insects; I meant microphones. I was so scared that I wet the bed. My mom panicked! She made me take a shower. While I was showering, she called a friend who suggested she drive me to The Ohio State University and be assessed in the emergency room. While driving to OSU, I crouched below the dashboard in the front seat and made my mom recite a prayer the whole time we drove.

I was immediately admitted to the psychiatric unit of OSU, Upham Hall. The staff at OSU were gentle and kind. I thought cameras were watching me, so they gave me a blanket to cover myself as we walked from the ER to Upham Hall. The paranoia only got worse. I thought the patients were not patients but people placed there to kill me.

The next day my mother visited me and I yelled, "She is not my mother! She is an imposter. Get her out of here!"

This was the first of fifteen hospitalizations in a psychiatric unit or hospital. Upham Hall was somewhat dingy and cold. Most of the patients were depressed and wandered the halls or sat in front of the TV not watching. Christmas was close, and the halls were decorated with paper snowflakes, red and green ribbons, and a fake Christmas tree. My room held two beds. The floor in the bedroom was cold and the lighting was irritating. I frequently sat in a rocking chair near a bird in a cage that became agitated when I sat down. The staff knew that this behavior from the bird was a sign of distress in me. An intern sat across from me with one hand casually held behind his back. I yelled, "You have scissors behind your back, don't you? You are going to kill me!"

I ran into my bedroom and attempted to flip my bed over. Four staff members picked me up, put me on a mattress on the floor of another room, and shot me in the butt with a sedative. One of the male staff members had his knee on my neck to keep me from spitting or biting. I was knocked out within seconds. When I awoke, I was in a dark room with the door open. Light was shining in from the hallway. I walked out of the room and a very kind woman was sitting in a chair outside the door reading a book.

"Are you hungry?" she asked.

"Yes," I said.

"What would you like?"

"Yogurt sounds good?"

She promptly got up, went to the front of the unit where there was a refrigerator, and brought me two containers of yogurt. I ate them quickly and asked for one more. This time she returned with peanut butter crackers and yogurt. The paranoia was much less severe. I stayed a week and was placed on anti-psychotic medication.

A month later, I slipped into a clinical depression. The symptoms were worse than before. This time I was suicidal.

I met with my first psychiatrist at age twenty. She was in her fifties and had a friendly smile. She graduated from the same high school I graduated from, CSG. This gave me comfort. Her office was in a high rise across the street from Grant Hospital. She tried many medications to relieve the depression, but to no avail. During one session she said, "Julie, you have had two clinical depressions and one psychotic break. This does not necessarily mean you have bipolar disorder, but I am treating you with medication that is specifically for the treatment of bipolar."

I worked with her for three years. During the three years I was hospitalized five times for depression. One of the last times I talked to her I was suicidal. I bought a gun while drunk the night before, and I called her in the morning and told her I had a loaded gun pointed at my head. She first told me to bring the gun to her office, but then she changed her mind and told me to take it to my father's office. I took it to his office and returned home. The last time I met with this psychiatrist she explained how to shoot myself to commit suicide. She said, "If you are going to use a gun to commit suicide, put the gun in your mouth and point it down your throat. Don't point it at your head." I didn't know how to react. Did she want me dead?

My parents began the search for a new psychiatrist.

Chapter Six
HANDCUFFS AND SUBTRACT 7 FROM 100

IN 1984, I was twenty-three, living with my father, and completing a bachelor's degree in Theology at Capital University. Capital was a small school in Bexley, Ohio, a mile from the Columbus School for Girls. I experienced my first manic episode.

My dad and I were having dinner at one of my favorite restaurants, Lindey's. The food was good and I enjoyed the live music. He could tell I was becoming unhinged because I would not stop talking. I also felt the beginnings of paranoia. I thought the band leader was an old boyfriend and tried to talk to him about our past relationship. My dad tried to convince me that I did not know this man, but I would not believe him. He quickly got me out of the restaurant and headed home.

When we got home, I told him I was going to drive to a friend's house and spend the night. He took my car keys away from me and went to bed. In my paranoid state, I thought he was going to kill me.

I grabbed an extra set of keys, ran out the door with a golf club, and ran to our neighbor's house. It was past midnight. The neighbor took me to my mother's house, about two miles away, and dropped me off. He was pissed and even said, "I knew there was something wrong going on in your house."

My mom immediately recognized that I was paranoid. She could not calm me down, and I was trying to convince her that Dad was trying to kill me. She called my older brother and an ambulance. An ambulance, police officer, and my brother arrived at the same time. I hid in my mom's shower. The police officer found me, handcuffed me, and guided me into the back of the ambulance. I was acting erratically and saying things that made absolutely no sense. A police officer sat in the back of the ambulance with me.

I said, "You have five children, don't you? You went to school at Otterbein before you became a police officer. Your wife's name is Sally."

He began sweating. "Have we met before? How could you know these things? This is scary."

I believe that when I get manic, I have access to more of my brain and become somewhat psychic. Every time I get manic I know things that should be impossible for me to know.

Instead of being taken to a general hospital ER for assessment, my mom directed them to take me to Harding Hospital. Harding is a free-standing private psychiatric hospital in Columbus. The ambulance drivers, the police officer, my mom, and my brother followed me into the admission building. First thing, one of the nurses angrily said, "Take the handcuffs off her! Now!"

I was too agitated to be assessed. The nurse took me into the general living area of the hospital unit where patients were watching TV, eating, and chatting with staff. I noticed a glassed-in area where people were smoking. The noise of the living area was too stimulating. The paranoia got worse. A nurse and doctor guided me to a room and said, "This is the quiet room. We will leave the door open, but we would like you to stay in here where it will be less stimulating."

The room was very small and consisted of a bed and a bathroom. The door was heavy and had a very small window in it. After ten minutes I left the room and tried to engage the staff and patients. This time, two psych technicians and a nurse guided me back to the quiet room and strapped me to the bed. I was in five-point restraints. My hands were cinched down to the side with no room to move, and my legs were also cinched down. There was a leather belt around my waist holding me firmly to the bed. They left the room. I yelled, screamed, and tried to move. No one came in. I noticed that every once in a while someone would peek through the small window in the door. This experience came too close to mimicking being locked in my bedroom as a kid. My paranoia heightened into delusions and hallucinations. The isolation was causing an increase in intensity of my symptoms. I don't know how long I was in there, but eventually someone came into the room and tried to talk to me.

"How are you feeling?"

I laughed and said, "What are you doing here? You should be out on the driving range teaching golf."

I thought he was the golf pro from the country club where I was taking lessons. In reality, he was the psychiatrist assigned to my care.

"Could you tell someone that I have to use the bathroom?" I said.

A nurse was called in carrying a bed pan. I said, "There is no way in hell I am using a bed pan!"

I convinced them I was not going to hurt anyone or run out of the room. They unlocked the restraints and allowed me to use the bathroom. When I was finished, they tied me back down to the bed.

When my symptoms abated, I was allowed out of the room and assigned a private room. Harding was cushy compared to OSU. There was carpet on the floor in the bedroom and a private shower and bathroom. The staff were kind and it seemed like they enjoyed their jobs.

One evening, while I was showering, my favorite nurse hid my slippers under my pillow. I came out of the shower and could not find the slippers.

"Where are they?"

"Where are what?"

"My slippers."

"Keep looking."

I am not the most patient or thorough person in the world. He had to tell me where they were.

This same favorite nurse said something I will never forget. I was in a fetal position facing away from the living room when the nurse came up behind me and said, "Let's shoot hoops." He had a basketball in his hand.

"I don't feel like doing anything," I said.

"If you change your mind, I will be outside," he said.

I dragged myself off the couch and joined him. We shot around for a while. "I feel better," I said.

He replied, "Remember this moment because if you can feel better, you can get better. When you are feeling at your worst, remember playing basketball with me and remember it helped."

The third day I was there, I was called into the office of one of the psychiatrists for an assessment. There were five interns also sitting in his office.

He said, "I would like you to subtract seven from one hundred and keep doing that until you can't think of the next number."

I stopped at ninety-three. *What the hell!* I was coming off mania, I was depressed, my mind was scattered, and he wanted me to do math. I was embarrassed to have to stop at ninety-three with the interns watching me. I couldn't do the test at that time.

I was a patient at Harding Hospital for seven months. Treatment consisted of activities, meeting with my therapist two times a week, and attending group therapy three times a week. The group therapy was held in the basement. It was dingy and made of cinder block. It made my depression worse just by entering the room. There were six patients in the group who rarely said anything. My therapist and a social worker monitored the group. I would say they ran the group, but in true psychoanalytic style, they never said anything.

I had a powerful exchange with one of the patients during group. His name was Joe. He was a professor at The Ohio State University. His hands were wrapped in gauze because he purposely burned them. One morning during group, I said, "How can anyone help us? We sit here three times a week, and none of the professionals suggest anything or say anything. Sam, are you in pain?" Up to this point, Sam said nothing.

He responded, "No more pain than anyone else in the room."

"So why don't you talk about it?"

He didn't answer me. I never saw Sam in group again. He was discharged the next day. If I had known he was planning to be discharged, I would have engaged him more.

My Analyst's Underwear

During my seven-month stay at Harding, my father sent fresh-cut flowers every Friday. They would appear around noon wrapped in colorful paper or a glass vase. Many times the flowers were roses of different colors. It was a nice gesture, but I hated it. It separated me from the other patients, and the flowers made me feel like I was his lover. Many times I gave them to other patients to brighten their rooms. One Friday in the spring, he sent a dozen red roses in a glass vase. This time I decided to keep them. I said to a staff member, "I'm not feeling well today. I think I will stay in my room and rest."

I took the flowers into my room, shut the door, and decided today was the day I would commit suicide. I took the flowers out of the vase, laid them on my bed, wrapped a washcloth around the vase, and began hitting the sink with the vase. This created shards of glass sharp enough to cut my wrists. I felt no ambivalence or interest in what I was doing. I made my decision and had every intention of carrying it out. I lay down on my side on my bed and began digging into my wrists with a particularly sharp shard. I dug into my left wrist but could not get blood to flow. I switched hands and again, I couldn't dig deep enough to cause the blood to spurt out. I had horrible gashes on both wrists. A nurse knocked on my door and said, "Your appointment with your therapist is in five minutes."

"OK, thank you. I'll be right out."

I put on a long-sleeve shirt. I felt stupid that I couldn't kill myself within the hour I had allotted myself. I took the stairs to my therapist's office and sat down. He didn't say anything, nor did I.

Finally I said, "I have done something to myself, but I don't want you to think I am trying to get attention. OK?"

"OK," he said.

I pulled up my sleeves and revealed the gashes in my wrists. There was very little blood. He immediately reached for the phone. I repeated, "I did not do this for attention. I really wanted to kill myself."

His eyes were huge, and again he said, "OK."

I was taken to another part of the hospital and sewed up. The psychiatrist who was called to sew up my wrists said to the interns who were watching, "This is only superficial. John, would you like to take a crack at sewing her right wrist?"

I interpreted what he said about my wounds being superficial as, "She wasn't really trying to kill herself. She just wanted attention."

The next day, a nurse was changing the dressing on my wrists and said, "Julie, if you are serious about killing yourself, cut lengthwise down your arm, not across."

I said, "Gee thanks. I'll remember that the next time I slit my wrists."

I was discharged against medical advice one week later. I was getting nowhere.

Chapter Seven
THE MENNINGER CLINIC

IN THE FALL OF 1988, I was clinically depressed again. After ten years of experiencing symptoms of mental illness, I was getting worse. The depressions were taking longer to pull out of, and I was having more periods of mania. Not one medication made a dent in depression or mania. There was one last ditch possibility. One of my sister's therapists suggested we contact the Menninger Clinic in Topeka, Kansas. The clinic was known for treating difficult mental illnesses. We were advised that it was very expensive, but my dad agreed to pay. There was a one-month waiting period. I spent most of that time either in bed or sitting in front of the TV not watching it.

My mom helped me pack a suitcase and we left for Topeka via plane in September 1988. I was numb. My thoughts ranged from, *This will be the place I will kill myself*, to, *Protect my family from finding me*, to *What if they can actually help me*. As we were preparing for landing, my mom and I heard the stewardess say, "Welcome to Kansas City, Missouri."

Kansas City, Missouri? I thought we would land in Kansas. We figured out that Kansas City, Missouri and Kansas City, Kansas were next to each other, and the airport was in Missouri. We took a two-engine airplane from the Kansas City airport to a small airport in Topeka. We stayed in a Holiday Inn across from the Menninger Clinic. I remember looking out the window and seeing a towering building with a clock. I remember thinking that this was where I would kill myself.

We met with the social worker and psychiatric nurse assigned to me. The room was small and stuffy. The social worker asked if I had questions. I said, "I am afraid I am becoming institutionalized. I have been hospitalized so many times."

The social worker said, "I understand your fear. I can't say for sure if that could happen. You will be participating in activities outside the unit, you will see your psychiatrist twice a week, and we are currently looking for a therapist to work with you while you are in the hospital."

His response did not help. I knew the gig. I would be assigned some stupid activities during the day and molt at night, confined to the unit.

The first two weeks at the clinic I was bombarded with psychological testing. Everything from the Rorschach test to telling stories about a picture that was shown to me. One picture was of a mother holding her child and the child was crying. My interpretation was that it was a child who was angry that she could not go outside because the mother had too many other children to take care of. After an interpretation I was always asked, "Is there more?"

I always said, "No."

My stories were pathetic. Depression takes all creativity and unique thought from me, causing me to tell very boring stories. For the entirety of those two weeks, a woman sat in the corner of the room reading a paperback book, or she pretended to. I later learned that she was the test taker's supervisor. Her name was Dr. Cerney. The name meant nothing to me, and I was irritated that she was listening in on my stupid storytelling.

After two weeks, I chose four activities out of eight that I thought I might like. I was still clinically depressed and could barely get out of bed, but once out of bed, the staff kept me moving. My favorite activity was woodworking. The first day I entered the woodworking building, I was overwhelmed by the smell of sawdust. The room was huge. There were pieces of logs, long planks, and many machines. Everyone was wearing goggles and hard at work. The teacher walked up to me and said, "Hi, Julie. I'm glad you chose this class. The first thing we ask new people to do is make a cutting board."

She had me watch the process of another patient making the cutting board and then left me on my own. I sanded and rounded six pieces of wood, painted them with glaze, and glued the pieces together. I thought I did a pretty good job. However, in my ADHD way, I did not glue the pieces in a straight way, nor did I put the pieces of wood in a line with the lightest wood first, followed by the next lightest wood. My cutting board looked very different than everyone else's. I felt embarrassed, but the teacher saw what I did . She quickly corrected the gluing and said, "Hey, I like the way you put the pieces of wood together. It is uniquely you."

The last project I worked on was a walking stick. The teacher pointed to a very large log and described how to turn it into a walking stick. The first thing I did was use a machine that stripped off the bark. I then used another machine to trim it into a thinner piece of log. The final and most tedious part was sanding the log into a two-inch-wide walking stick. I sanded that log for months. The teacher encouraged me to keep sanding, but eventually I could sand no more. It currently sits in the corner of my apartment as a reminder of the hard work I was able to do while still depressed.

I met one of my best friends in woodworking. He and I would sneak outside the building and smoke. He was Jewish, from Arizona, and he made me laugh. He was a good storyteller. His family was very wealthy, and a couple of years ago his mother was kidnapped and put in the trunk of a car. She was later found after the family paid a ransom. I never asked why he was there. This was true of all of my hospitalizations. No one ever asked why the other person was in the hospital.

One of the other activities was group therapy. I audibly groaned when the activities therapist told me this was a required activity. Really? Another boring hour and a half of people sitting in a dingy room saying nothing? It turned out to be quite different. Group was held in a room surrounded by windows with grass and trees visible. There were seven patients in the room, and three to four clinicians acted as our guides. I always sat in the same place, and to the dismay of the clinicians, leaned my chair back on its two legs. We were given fifteen minutes to speak. There was no particular order in which we spoke, but the clinicians kept track of who last spoke. Group therapy at Menninger was very different than group therapy at Harding. The clinicians actually interacted with us. A patient might say, "This has been a really bad day."

The clinician might respond, "Can you say more about that?"

I kept many of my thoughts to myself when other people spoke.

Depression made me very critical internally, either against myself or others. While halfway listening to an exchange between a patient and a psychiatrist, I was called upon to offer my thoughts and feelings about what was being said.

I said, "I wasn't listening."

The psychiatrist said, "Why weren't you listening?"

"I turned the conversation off in my head when the insanity of what was being discussed made me angry."

The psychiatrist said, "What made you angry?"

The psychiatrist and I went around in circles about me telling her what I heard and why I would not share. In frustration I said, "Fine. This is what I am thinking. Susie is being treated for an eating disorder, and you are encouraging her to work with a nurse who is morbidly obese. It would be like me trying to stay sober and my therapist showing up drunk to every session with him." The nurse I was referring to was in the room. I didn't dare look at her.

The room became silent. The psychiatrist who had encouraged me to speak looked at the clock said, 'Well, our time is up."

The clinicians left the room.

After they left the room and the door was closed, we all broke into laughter. I wasn't attempting to be mean. I told the psychiatrist I did not want to share, but she pushed me. The patient who had the eating disorder told me she was grateful that someone finally said what she had been thinking since being assigned to this nurse.

Chapter Eight
THE BEGINNING OF A SIX-YEAR PSYCHOANALYTIC RELATIONSHIP

IT TOOK FOUR MONTHS to find a psychoanalyst to take my case. I was never told why, but I think it was because someone with issues as complicated as mine caused analysts to avoid working with me. Psychoanalysis requires someone with a strong sense of self. A strong ego is needed. The ego is part of the mind that mediates between the conscious and unconscious. Ego is responsible for reality testing and a sense of personal identity. Psychoanalysis could cause a break in the ego leading to psychosis. I had been psychotic so many times, and that could have been the reason psychoanalysts felt psychoanalysis was the wrong way to help me heal. Fortunately, the director of the unit in which I lived felt different. He told the staff that nothing in the past had worked, and he felt analysis might make the difference between continuing to decompensate or heal. He felt the psychological testing revealed a strong ego.

The director of the unit asked Dr. Cerney if she would be willing to have me as a psychoanalytic patient. I was told her response was, "I was waiting for you to ask me."

Our first session began the first week of January 1989. A staff member walked me to Dr. Cerney's office and left me in the waiting room. It was 7:00 a.m. and no one else was in the building. I sat down and saw a light coming out of an office. The building was cold. Out of the darkness, Dr. Cerney approached and led me to her office. She sat down first. I looked around and saw books everywhere. Books were piled high on her desk, on the floor, beside her chair, and they filled a huge bookcase that wrapped around the room. She had a neutral look on her face, but warmth emanated from her. A staff member told me she was a Franciscan nun. Two of my aunts were nuns and I always felt loved by them.

I said, "Should I sit down or lie on the couch?"

"That's up to you."

I sat in the chair and looked her over. Sitting in the chair she appeared tall and sat very upright. She was wearing a brownish dress, hose, and high-heeled shoes that matched her dress. Her hair was long and she wore it in a style similar to a beehive. I guessed she was in her mid-sixties. I was still very depressed and had very little confidence in her. I had confidence in no one at this point.

I said, "There is one thing that is very important to me."

She waited.

"You must stay within the boundaries of the therapeutic relationship."

Her eyes became very large and she said, "Of course. Why is that important to you?"

I said, "I have been in too many therapeutic relationships where the therapist felt more like my friend than the person treating me. I used to see one of my psychiatrists at the country club pool and I would play with her children. It was terribly inappropriate, but there was nothing we could do. She took her kids to the pool, I was there, and I interacted with the family as if I were part of the family. As I look back now, I realize how wrong that was. I don't blame myself. She played a part in it."

Dr. Cerney had a tendency to speak cryptically and in very short sentences. She rarely answered a question. One of her sayings was, "What do you think about that?" Sometimes it pissed me off. I would ask her a direct question and she would turn it back to me. I learned early on that this was the style of psychoanalysis. Dr. Cerney wrote everything I said in a stenographer's book. I know that because after she died, I requested the pads. I had to file a petition with the court to be given the pads. Menninger staff wanted to hand them over to my general practitioner. I did not have a GP and knew that any medical file related to me was mine.

I remember very little of what we talked about. She was silent when I spoke. One day I was feeling better and plopped down on the couch.

She said, "You're going to break the couch."

I wasn't sure if she was kidding, but joking around was not her style with me.

She said, "Of course." That was all she usually said.

I can only remember one other time she spoke. I was no longer required to move around campus with a staff member, and I was given the privilege of not only walking around the campus by myself, but I could go off grounds and explore Topeka. I started jogging around town. The minute the doors were unlocked in the morning, I was out the door and headed into town. I built up enough endurance to jog an hour. One of the nurses saw me jogging miles from the campus and expressed concern. Dr. Cerney told me this and said, "They are all just jealous that you can jog so far."

Jogging was critical to my healing. I was still depressed, but I knew that if I could get back to jogging, like in high school, I could stir up endorphins and ease the pain. It absolutely made a big difference. The depression began to lift, and I could enjoy activities and people again. A male nurse on the unit would always bend down, before I jogged, and tie my shoes. One morning I bent over to tie my shoes and thought, *Wow, I can tie my shoes without it feeling difficult.* That's how intense my depression was. The simple act of bending over and tying my shoes hurt.

As I began to feel better, I began to talk more. I told Dr. Cerney of my dreams. I told her about my siblings and parents. I told her I wanted to go back to school and attempt to get into law school. I even mentioned my fantasy of having a boyfriend. I began to depend heavily on our morning sessions. There were times I told her I hated her for not talking to me, yet turned around the next day and wanted to be symbiotically connected to her. I struggled to not feel too attached to her for fear she would think I was healed and stop seeing me. If she ever took a vacation, I felt like a baby searching for a nipple to feed me.

I have read through the stenographer pad more than once, hoping to find a private response to something I might have said. There were very few notes expressing her thoughts. True to analytic form, she only wrote what I said, except twice that I can remember. I was crying and she wrote: "She was crying."

Another time she spoke was on a cold February morning, five months after analysis started. I got up at 6:00 a.m. and went out to my car, but it wouldn't start. The temperature was in the single digits. I decided to jog the four miles to her office. By the time I got there, I was close to hypothermia. I lay down on the couch and was shaking uncontrollably. She said, "There is a blanket at the end of the couch."

I thought, *Then put it on me.*

We both waited to see what would happen next. She got up out of her chair and draped the blanket over me. I was shocked! She actually got out of her chair. That never happened before.

I know this may sound like a cold form of therapy, but it wasn't. I entered her office and it was like being on a warm island, just the two of us, sitting on a beach and me telling her of my past, present, and hopes and dreams. I fell deeply in love with her.

I also began having strong feelings for the nurse who tied my shoes every morning. He stood about five feet eleven inches tall, had a strong body and a beautiful grin. One day I returned from activities and there was a small potted plant placed on the ledge of my window. He began sneaking in my room and watering it. He would knock on my door every morning and say, "Julie, it's time to light the candle and get a move on."

Christmas of 1988, I returned from activities and found a pair of red and blue festive Christmas socks lying on my bed. This was a boundary violation as defined by Menninger, but he noticed I had holes in my socks and felt compelled to get me new ones. When he was on duty and I was not at activities, we were together doing errands around campus or sitting in the dayroom talking. Every time a client left the unit, they had to sign out. I was sitting on the patio reading the paper and the male nurse came out and said, "C'mon. It's a beautiful day. Let's do errands around here and walk the trail."

I jumped up with excitement. When we returned to the unit, the staff were in a frenzy. He had forgotten to sign me out. He never took ownership of the mistake and blamed it on me. Due to this infraction, I was confined to the unit for four days. Dr. Cerney was out of town and I had to wait for her to return before I was taken off confinement. I was livid. All of my privileges were restricted and I had to molt on the unit. I went to my room, lay on my bed, and shut my eyes, damning him. He walked into my room and apologized.

He said, "Julie! Please look at me. I am so sorry. I could have gotten into a lot of trouble if they thought I forgot to sign you out."

I said, "So instead you decided to get me into trouble. I can't even go outside!" I did not open my eyes.

He continued to beg me to look at him, but I wouldn't. I couldn't. He was the cause of my unit confinement. When Dr. Cerney returned, the confinement was lifted. It took a month for me to trust him again.

I began to heal. I was able to experience emotions dampened by depression. I was prescribed many medications with no results. When I was discharged in November 1989, I was taking Lithium. My diagnosis at discharge was bipolar disorder, in remission, and depression, in remission. I was rated "low" on level of functioning. I took myself off Lithium a week after discharge. It made me shake and I did not think it was making a difference in how I felt. The clinical depression was gone, and I felt ready to be on my own. I lived in Kansas for thirteen years and never had a manic episode or suffered another depression. I actually felt I was cured. That was to be a big flaw in my thinking.

Chapter Nine
DISCHARGE FROM THE MENNINGER CLINIC

I CONTINUED ANALYSIS with Dr. Cerney five days a week. We always met at 7:00 a.m. My father decided he was no longer going to pay for treatment. He was paying cash and the cost began to be a problem. He and his wife were building a home on the coast of Key Largo and he needed the money. All I had with me was a suitcase filled with clothes and my Volvo. I had no idea where I was going to live. A week before discharge, I was crying because I didn't know where to look for housing. Dr. Cerney suggested I call Most Pure Heart of Mary Church, where she played the organ, and ask if anyone was renting an apartment. As luck would have it, an elderly member of the church rented me a very small apartment attached to her home. It was perfect. The apartment was fully furnished. The kitchen consisted of a sink, toaster oven, and small refrigerator. I applied for disability before I was discharged and received $310 a month. The rent was exactly $310.

My Analyst's Underwear

I knew no one in the Topeka community, but I knew exactly where I wanted to work part-time. While in the hospital, staff and patients took a trip to The Meat and Cheese Shop. The owner had been a patient at Menninger years ago. I liked the feel of the shop and felt I could handle the work. After discharge, I approached the owner and asked for a job. I had no resume or references. I told him I was a past patient at Menninger. He shared part of his story and hired me on a probationary basis. He said if I proved I could handle the work he would keep me on board. I thrived from that point forward.

I worked from 4–8:00 p.m., four times a week. My father was sending me a little bit of money. With that and the little I was making at the shop, I got by. I managed a cash register, shaved meat for sandwiches, cleaned, and talked to customers about what kind of cheeses they were interested in buying. I loved the work. It kept me out of my apartment and engaged with others. When I got home, I put on my jogging shoes and ran through the streets of Topeka for an hour. I loved running by the zoo. I could hear the roar of the lions and tigers. The rest of my time was spent meeting with Dr. Cerney and exploring the small town of Topeka. I began to play golf by myself, but there were times when I was paired with other people. My favorite course was the Lake Shawnee Golf Course. It wound around the beautiful lake. There were times I spent hours on the driving range waking up my muscle memory. I bought an old classical guitar and a Christopher Parkening book and took three lessons. I spent hours practicing and became pretty good. For two years, this was my life. I was stable and still on no medication. I didn't make friends until I moved out of the apartment and got a new job.

I was getting bored and felt I could handle more responsibilities. I saw an ad in the *Topeka Capital Journal* looking for someone to manage a program for mentally ill people who were homeless. The program provided housing. I got the job and began my first forty-hour-a-week job. I felt like it was time to give back because I was given so much. My days were spent helping clients shop for groceries and helping them interact with other people. It was a challenging two years. It was difficult finding affordable housing for clients who were on disability. After two years, I decided to find a job that paid more and offered me a chance to help in a different way. I applied to work at the Ronald McDonald House in Topeka. I was on call from 11:00 p.m.–7:00 a.m. They provided me with a house that had a phone that rang directly from the phone attached to the outside of the Ronald McDonald House. If a family came in late, they would call me and I would walk over and let them in. The job was easy. I did laundry, mowed the lawn, and greeted guests. Since I was making more money, I decided to take psychology classes at Washburn University. I could walk to the university from where I lived.

While playing tennis with an acquaintance from my job, the tennis director came out of her office and said, "What is in your water bottles?"

He and I looked at each other, confused, and I answered, "Water."

I remember the day so clearly. It was beautiful, the sky was deep blue, there was a slight breeze, and the temperature was about 75. He and I were horrible players. The tennis balls were flying everywhere. I later learned the director thought we were drunk. She became my first true friend in Topeka. Her name was Charlotte and she was married. She was laid back, funny, and a great coach. When I wasn't working or taking classes, I was with Charlotte. She gave me my first of many tennis lessons. I was not a natural tennis player, but I was an athlete. The skills of previous sports gave me a leg up on learning quickly. I absolutely loved playing tennis and began developing a strong swing. I could not hit a forehand top spin and my backhand was a one-arm slice, but Charlotte helped me make it work.

After an indoor lesson, Charlotte and I were relaxing and watching others play. I noticed a man playing tennis as if he were a professional. He was beautiful, thin, and moved quickly around the court. I asked Charlotte, "Who is that guy in the white shirt playing great tennis?"

Charlotte said, "Oh my god! Why didn't I think of this? That's Kurt. He is in the middle of a divorce. You two would make a great couple."

I didn't see him again until spring. He was teaching tennis to a group of women. I was watching how good he was at identifying a weakness in a player and quickly helping them adjust their swing. He began noticing me watching him. I told Dr. Cerney about Kurt and expressed a wish to get to know him. Dr. Cerney said little. I wondered if I was ready for a boyfriend. I never had an adult intimate relationship. I was thirty-two and had not had intercourse. I was too sick for the intimacy of a physical relationship. I also had a rule about relationships. The rule was to never date anyone unless they had been divorced for two years. Kurt had been separated for a year but was not yet divorced. My rule was about to be broken.

I became good enough at tennis to become a member of the United States Tennis Association (USTA). I was rated 3.0. The ratings ranged from 2.0–open. An open rating meant you were the top player and could play in any tournament. I began playing in local tournaments and won more than I lost. On a clear summer Saturday, I won the first round of a tournament held at the Tennis Center in Topeka. I was exhilarated. As I walked off the court, I noticed Kurt leaning against the fence. He said, "Good job. Your tennis has improved."

He noticed me playing?!

I knew he won his first round too and said, "You're not so bad yourself."

That's all it took. From that point forward, we spent as much time as we could together. He would stop by the Ronald McDonald House and bring me cherry slushies. He worked at Goodyear as a manager and talked about his day. He began teaching me a stronger form of tennis. He was an excellent coach, and I was a good student. I was completely entranced. I could not believe that I might finally be ready for a boyfriend.

Chapter Ten
THE GREATEST TIME OF MY LIFE

OUR RELATIONSHIP moved slowly. The only physical contact we had in the first month was hugging. I clearly remember our first kiss. We were sitting on the floor in the living room at my house at The Ronald McDonald House. He moved toward me, and as he did, I moved toward him. His eyes were bright blue and very alive. He leaned in and kissed me. After kissing, we moved back and looked each other straight in the eyes. It was the best kiss I ever tasted. The next kiss lasted much longer. From that point forward, we began to explore each other's bodies. He was in excellent shape. His arms were tight and muscular from playing tennis. His legs were strong, especially his thighs. He touched me in places I had never been touched. I never pulled away. His touch was gentle. When he left one of our marathon explorations of the body, I felt high. I couldn't wait to see him again.

Kurt and I spent a lot of time playing tennis and jogging. Fun had returned to my life. One night he called at 8:30 p.m. and asked me to meet him at the tennis courts with my tennis racquet. It was dark, but I asked no questions.

He was waiting for me in the parking lot when I got there. He said, "Let's play tennis."

"In the dark?"

"Watch," he said.

He moved to an electrical panel, opened the metal cover, and flipped a switch. The courts lit up! We were the only ones on the courts. It was magical. We laughed because the tennis balls flew into the dark night and we would hit them the moment they hit the court. We played for an hour. We were sweaty and exhilarated. I followed him to the electrical panel, and just before turning off the lights, he hugged and kissed me. I did not sleep well that night. The fun kept running through my head. I wondered if someone in a helicopter or low-flying plane would look down, see the lights and wonder what was going on.

He introduced me to his friends and family. He had two daughters who spent the weekends with him during the divorce. His father was a former football coach and very accepting of me. I loved his mom. She was funny and took me in as if I were one of her four children. The relationship with Kurt gave me the confidence to reach out to other people. I was playing tennis on the weekends with women who were on our USTA team. We traveled throughout the state to play in tournaments. I won many of my singles matches. By the time I left Topeka, thirteen years later, I was on the cusp of being rated 4.5 by the USTA. I never felt better, physically and mentally.

One evening, after Kurt left, I was cleaning the dishes in the kitchen and heard someone being interviewed on the 10 o'clock news. I stopped cleaning and went into the living room, listening to the woman being interviewed. She sounded strong and confident. She was a legislator in Topeka. I don't remember what she said, but I thought how little I knew about politics. I went to bed thinking I would contact her in the morning and ask if she needed someone to volunteer for her.

In the morning, I called her legislative office and she answered, "This is Kathleen Sebelius."

"Mrs. Sebelius, my name is Julie Brown. I saw you interviewed on the news last night. I was wondering if you could use volunteer help?"

"Absolutely. Call my friend Joyce. She will give you an idea of the research we need. Thank you for calling."

We hung up and I called Joyce. She explained to me what was needed. She said not to rush, but I got the work done in three days. That was how anxious I was to begin volunteering. I was attending classes in the morning and still working at the Ronald McDonald House, but I found the time to complete the task.

A couple weeks later, Joyce called me and said she would like to meet with me. I invited her to join me in the library at the Ronald McDonald House. When she walked in the library, I closed the doors and we sat down. She said, "No one knows this yet, but Kathleen is thinking about running for the office of Commissioner of Insurance. She needs a team of people to help. She would be the first female and first Democrat to ever attempt winning this office."

I didn't say anything. I couldn't imagine what she was going to say next. Was she asking for money? Would she change her mind if she knew I was a former Menninger patient?

She said, "We need someone to be a volunteer coordinator or scheduler. Do either of these positions interest you?"

She explained what each position would require. I couldn't imagine I would be good at scheduling Kathleen's days for a year. I knew nothing about Kansas and felt overwhelmed by the thought of being responsible for where and when Kathleen would campaign.

I said, "I have no idea. I know nothing about politics. Would you give me a day to talk to someone about each position?"

She was pleased I asked the question. She felt it showed I was smart enough not to jump into the campaign too quickly.

I called my older brother's wife. Her father was in politics and I felt she might have an idea about what this might require. It didn't take her long to suggest I might like being a scheduler rather than organizing volunteers. I called Joyce back and told her of my decision to help with scheduling. I thought it was a great way to learn about politics. She sounded pleased. Joyce was an amazing mentor. She moved swiftly and with precision. She was the perfect campaign director. She instilled confidence in me and guided me throughout the year.

This was the first time in my life that I enjoyed every minute. The best part about it was that I created it. No one could take anything from me. My work had nothing to do with my status in the community, where I attended school, or knowing the right people. I was on no medication and had not been manic or depressed since discharge from Menninger in November 1989, five years ago.

Chapter Eleven
THE CAMPAIGN TRAIL

AS THE CAMPAIGN WORE ON, I learned more about Kathleen. She was born in Cincinnati, Ohio. Her father, John Gilligan, was Governor of Ohio in the early seventies. She married Gary Sebelius in the governor's mansion in Bexley, Ohio. When they married, I was attending the Columbus School for Girls a mere mile from the governor's mansion. Gary's father had been a senator in western Kansas. Gary and Kathleen met in DC and moved to Topeka. Gary was a lawyer and worked in a law firm downtown. They had two children. I remember seeing a picture in the paper of Kathleen sitting in her legislative office with one of her sons lying in a baby carrier next to her desk.

Joyce found a campaign office not far from the state capitol. The space consisted of one large room, a bathroom, and a smaller room where Kathleen could conduct private business. The center of the room was lined with heavy metal tables covered in paperwork and envelopes. We had a couple of computers that were basically used as word processors. We had a fundraiser, volunteer coordinator, press guy, campaign director, and the candidate. We hit the ground running.

The path to Kathleen becoming insurance commissioner was grueling. I went to classes in the morning, spent the afternoons and evening at the campaign office, and worked at the Ronald McDonald House at night. I had never worked so hard in my life, and I loved every minute of it. Kansas has traditionally voted Republican. We had our work cut out for us.

While planning the schedule for the day, I heard someone say, "Does the campaign car have insurance?"

The room went silent. A small voice from our press guy sheepishly said, "No."

We burst into laughter! How could we have forgotten this? There were so many details to attend to and this one fell through the cracks. We marched in parades, attended state fairs, and spent days on the road. I did not travel as often with Kathleen as I would have liked, due to my need to be close to the campaign office to keep the schedule rolling.

As election day bore down on us, we dug in even deeper. Kathleen attended more events and we were spending more time at the office. The polls were in our favor, but no one took that for granted. Kathleen was potentially unseating a male Republican incumbent preceded by all male Republican insurance commissioners. Election day made me nervous. After voting, I went to the campaign office and had nothing to do but wait. We all waited. There were two rooms being held at a local hotel for the post-election party. I wasn't feeling well, so Kathleen suggested I go to the hotel and relax. I got there and people were already preparing the room for a party. Food and drinks were being brought up by the hotel staff. I lay in bed wondering if the race would be called early. I couldn't believe we were at this point. One year of intense campaigning and it came down to one day of voting.

I did not have to wait long. The election was called before midnight. Kathleen was the new Insurance Commissioner of Kansas; the first woman and first Democrat! The hotel rooms were packed. Kathleen was being pulled in so many different directions. At one point, she did a phone interview with a Kansas City radio station in the bathroom because the rooms were so loud. I left the party around 1:30 a.m. There were so many thoughts going through my head. The most important being, *I can quit my job at the Ronald McDonald House and work at the Insurance Department.* That meant I would need to find a new place to live, get a nicer wardrobe, and think about what I might do at the Department. I wondered how this win would affect my relationship with Kathleen. Would she be too busy to hang out with me anymore? Would I see Joyce much anymore? What would happen to my campaign buddies? Everyone had big decisions to make.

The next day, I returned to the campaign office and found a $1,000 check on my desk. It was totally unexpected but gratefully appreciated.

A week or so after the election, the campaign team met and discussed what role each person would play at the department. I chose to work in the Consumer Assistance Division as a health insurance advocate. My job was to help Kansans resolve issues with their health insurance carrier. One of my biggest concerns, after the dust settled, was how I would fit in an hour of psychoanalysis every day with Dr. Cerney. I had held non-traditional jobs previous to working for the state, giving me time to meet with her. It was decided that I would get to work at 8:00 a.m., check out for an hour to meet with Dr. Cerney, and stay at work until 5:00 p.m.

I enjoyed my work at the Insurance Department. Working with insurance companies to resolve consumers' complaints was rewarding. This was a potential lifetime job. I never had a job before that I felt I could keep for a long time. However, I basically wanted to continue to support Kathleen in her professional and political pursuits. I did not know how far she wanted to go, or would go, but I wanted to be helpful. I remember playing golf with her one afternoon and she said, "Julie, if you could do anything you wanted, what would it be?"

"Actually, play golf, but since I am too old for that, I want to continue to support you in whatever direction you go."

She said, "I appreciate that, but I want you to find your own path. You are talented and have a life to develop based on your strengths."

I felt disappointed. I half thought she would agree with me and tell me she wanted me by her side the whole way. But she was right. I did need to contemplate how to direct my life.

Chapter Twelve
THE DEATH OF DR. CERNEY

But she is in her grave, and, oh
The difference to me.
—William Wordsworth

I HAD BEEN WORKING at the Insurance Department for less than a year when Dr. Cerney died on Monday, February 19, 1996. A few days before, on February 14, I decided to take a break. I flew to Key Largo, Florida, where my dad and his wife were building a home on the Atlantic. While the house was being built, they rented a condominium in a gated community called the Ocean Reef Club. My older sister and her husband and I met in Miami and drove to Key Largo. The new home would sit on stilts, have a beautiful tiled pool on the second floor, and overlook a calm ocean. There were no waves because there was a breaker about three miles from the coast that stopped the waves from hitting land. Florida was the perfect place to regenerate.

On the Tuesday after Dr. Cerney died, I played tennis with a member of the club. She beat me handily.

When I returned to my dad's place, he said, "How'd you do?"

"She beat me! I don't understand what happened. She had jewelry covering her body, she was at least fifteen years older than I am, and she beat me. Her jewelry would fly around as she hit the ball. I am embarrassed that I lost."

He laughed and said, "Oh, these people do this for a living. They ride around in their huge yachts, tie up for a day or two, and move on to the Virgin Islands and other clubs and live and breathe tennis and golf."

While we were talking, my sister and her husband walked onto the patio. My sister's eyes looked huge.

I said, "What's wrong?"

"Nothing. It was a long and hot jog."

My father said to me, "Let's go down to the dock and see if our resident shark is swimming around."

We walked down the short path and looked into the ocean water. He pulled me close to his side and said, "Doctor Cerney died yesterday."

"Dad, that's not funny. Don't joke about something like that."

"I'm not joking. Doctor B. called and said to call him at eleven o'clock. He wants to tell you what happened."

I immediately knew it was true. How could he have known Dr. B.'s name? My knees wobbled and I began to sway. I went into shock. Time completely slowed down and my mind went blank. Dad guided me to a chair on the dock and said, "When the church clock rings eleven times, you can call Doctor B."

I called Dr. B. at exactly 11:00 and said, "What happened?"

"Dr. Cerney's body was filled with cancer. It broke her back. She was very fond of you."

Fond of me? That's the best he could do?

He said the funeral would be in Topeka at Most Pure Heart of Mary Church the next day. I flew out of Miami that afternoon and headed to Topeka. I cried quietly the whole trip. There was a layover in St. Louis. The plane had technical difficulties that delayed the flight by three hours. I called people from the airport and told them of her death. I had to talk to anyone and everyone.

I arrived at the Kansas City Airport at 1:00 a.m. The shuttle to Topeka was not running due to the late hour. There was one cab driver smoking a cigarette not far from where I was standing. I asked her if she would drive me to Topeka, eighty minutes west. She said she had never driven to Topeka but was willing. I had exactly $100 in my wallet. I hoped it was enough to cover the cost of the trip. I said nothing to the cab driver. She tried to engage me in conversation, but I was still in shock and could think of nothing to say.

What was I going to do next? Wouldn't I need another analyst or therapist to help me grieve the loss? No one could possibly understand the depth of this loss. I remembered our last session and groaned audibly. "Fuck you" was the last thing I said to her.

The last year of her life, my senses were heightened because I knew she was in pain. She would shift around in her chair as if she could not get comfortable. During one session, I offered her a pillow off the couch and she accepted it. That's when I really got scared. Her acceptance of the pillow was so unlike her. She would never have accepted something from me unless she was hurting. I would sit on the edge of the couch and sob because I wanted her to get help. She referred my crying back to me. She said I was projecting and would not acknowledge her suffering.

One morning, I was waiting for her in my car in the parking lot. She drove up, popped the trunk, and began loading a luggage carrier with books. She was having trouble bending down to put the books on the carrier. I jumped out of my car and helped her with the books and dragged the carrier into her office. I was so confused. She was allowing me to do things for her in a way she never had before. Dr. B. said her back was eaten away by the cancer. This must have been the beginning of the cancer. She never once complained or groaned. She never once canceled a session.

My apartment was freezing. The building was heated with steam. I turned all the knobs on the radiators, and the smell and sound of steam poured into my apartment. I dropped my luggage and looked at my answering machine. There were thirteen messages. I was exhausted. I sat down on the floor in my bedroom and pushed the button to begin hearing the messages. The first one was from Kurt. We were not dating at that time. He said, "Julie, I am so sorry. If you need me, call me."

The second message was from Kathleen. She said, "Julie, when you get home, no matter what time, call me." She left one more message about an hour later saying the same thing. It was 3:00 a.m. I didn't call anyone back.

The rest of the messages were from tennis friends, coworkers, and family members. I cried through every message. I was overwhelmed by how much people cared about me. Everyone knew I was in Florida and didn't want me to read Dr. Cerney's obituary when I got home. I took a shower and lay on the couch. I had to be at work at 8:00 a.m. and I knew I would not sleep. As mundane as this sounds, I wondered what I would wear to her funeral. There is no protocol that dictates what to do when an analyst dies before the end of analysis. I was not a friend, member of her family, or a coworker. I loved her dearly, but I had no way of expressing that love. It wasn't like I was going to show up at a gathering of her circle of people and mourn the loss. No one I knew was in analysis. This was going to be a silent and lonely journey.

Chapter Thirteen
FUNERAL IN TOPEKA

I ARRIVED AT THE FUNERAL HOME at 6:00 p.m. The only people in the room were her siblings and some people who appeared to be friends. I sat down at the back of the funeral home and waited. I wasn't sure for what. I did not want to get close to the casket. It was open and I did not want to see her dead body. A psychiatrist friend arrived. He was the same person who told me she was dead when I was in Florida. He walked up to me and said, "Have you said your goodbye?"

"I can't go up to the casket. I don't want to see her dead."

He said, "Julie, you know what she taught you about dealing with grief. When the casket is open, a person has to prove the death by seeing them in the coffin. She would want you to say your final words to her, whether dead or alive."

"But the last thing I said to her was for her to fuck herself."

He said, "Further reason to address her directly."

I stood up. He held out his left arm and I put my arm on his. He led me to the coffin.

There was a kneeler beside the coffin. Dr. B. stepped back and sat down close to where I was kneeling.

I was unable to look at her face. I looked at what she was wearing and remembered her wearing that outfit weeks ago. I moved from looking at her dress to her hair. I still could not look at her face. Her hair was exactly as it was when she was alive. I finally looked at her face. *Wait*, I thought, *this isn't Dr. Cerney.* Her spirit was gone. She looked like someone I did not know. I felt panic. I kneeled in front of her for a very short time and started to sob. Her sister, Jeanette, rushed to my side and said, "Touch her hand."

Touch her hand? I had never touched her in the six years I was in analysis with her. She took my hand and started to move it toward Dr. Cerney when Dr. B. said, "Leave her alone."

Jeanette pulled back and my sobbing got louder. This time, her brother and sister-in-law moved toward me and stood beside me with their hands on my back. I didn't want anyone to touch me or be near me. This was a private moment. Jeanette leaned over Dr. Cerney and took an angel pin off Dr. Cerney's lapel and gave it to me. Just as she did this, the funeral director said, "It is time to move the body to the church. Services start soon."

I needed more time with her. I didn't want to forget what she looked like, even though she was dead. Move her body? That sounded so crass and insensitive. I stepped back from the kneeler, the casket was closed, and the funeral director wheeled her behind a door that he promptly shut. I felt completely empty. The tears were gone, but my emotions were raw. I began to feel the tiredness from lack of sleep for two days. I knew I had to get to the church and find a seat that would allow me to see everyone in the church and at the same time see her casket.

When I got there, the only people in the church were altar boys lighting candles and the priest preparing the front of the church for a funeral mass. I found a seat that would allow me to see everything. I knelt down and began praying a childhood prayer. *Hail Mary, full of Grace, the Lord is with thee. Blessed art thou among women; blessed is the fruit of thy womb Jesus. Holy Mary Mother of God, pray for us sinners now and at the hour of our death.* I brought Sister Mary Helen's rosary and began saying prayers. By the time I was finished with the rosary, people began to arrive. Within an hour, the church was packed. There were people standing at the back because there were not enough seats. The organist began practicing the songs. I only recognized staff from Menninger. The coffin was wheeled to the front of the church, followed by the priest and altar boys. I did not cry. I now knew this was the beginning of the end.

After mass, people gathered at the back of the church and outside. I had no patience or inclination to talk to anybody. I went home and made plans to fly to the funeral at her motherhouse in Tiffin, Ohio.

At 7:00 a.m. the next morning, I stopped in to work. I told my best friend I was leaving and would not be back for a couple of days. I informed the clerical staff that I should be back in the office by Monday. I didn't tell my supervisor where I was going. Kathleen knew I would be leaving. I tried to say goodbye to her but she was not in the office yet. I had to get to the airport for a noon flight. I was moving quickly. The shock passed. I packed a bag and headed for Kansas City International Airport.

Chapter Fourteen
FUNERAL IN TIFFIN, OHIO

I CALLED MY MOM before I left and asked her to pick me up at the airport in Columbus. When I walked through the gate, I started crying. She looked confused and maybe a little embarrassed. She drove me to Kevin's house. He and his wife were very kind and gracious. They made dinner for me and I played with the kids. The distraction was helpful. I didn't sleep that night. I was running on adrenalin. I felt like the shell of a person. I was anxious to get to Tiffin.

Early the next morning, Kevin let me borrow his car and I started the hour and a half drive to Tiffin. I was surprisingly calm. Cell phones were fairly new at this time. Kevin lent me the use of his cell phone, and all the way to Tiffin I called friends. I even called the psychologist who worked with me at Harding Hospital. His sonorous voice was soothing. He offered to meet with me when I returned to Columbus. He commented on how well I had done while at Menninger. I did not have time to meet with him after the funeral. I needed to get back to Topeka and be with friends to help me through the mourning.

    I arrived at the motherhouse at 10:30 a.m. It was gray outside and felt like it was about to rain. I entered the main building and was greeted by a sister. I said, "My name is Julie. I am here for the funeral of Sister Mary Cerney. She was my psychoanalyst for six years."

    She said, "The funeral is not until this evening. Would you like to pray in the chapel?"

    I thought, *No. I want to know where her body is and sit with her.* We entered the chapel and there were four sisters kneeled in prayer. I immediately saw the casket and it was open. The chapel had the smell of incense and lit candles. It was simple and beautiful. I found a place to sit where I could see her body. I did not pray. I couldn't think of anything. I just sat there and observed her in the casket.

    After forty-five minutes, a sister approached me and said, "I understand you are a former patient of Sister Mary. Would you like to meet one of her best friends?"

    She led me to a different building that housed the infirmary. We entered a small cold room. The first thing I noticed was a vase filled with fresh-cut flowers. The room smelled clean. The sister was bedridden. She was doing missionary work years ago and a porch collapsed under her, breaking her back. She showed no visible signs of pain. She appeared to have accepted her condition. We spoke quietly about Sister Mary's impact on her life. I commented on her beautiful flowers. She said, "Sister Mary sends me fresh flowers every week."

    I instantly knew what I was going to do. After I left her room, I asked someone where the flower shop was. I drove there and asked the owner to continue sending fresh-cut flowers to the sister every week. He set up an account and sent me a bill every month. I did this up until the sister died about a year later. It felt good to carry on Dr. Cerney's expression of love.

When I returned to the motherhouse that day, the sisters invited me to lunch. I was an outsider. They had no idea who I was, but their kindness and gentle care made me think, *What a beautiful place for Dr. Cerney to be buried.* We had a short lunch followed by empty time before the funeral that evening. I contemplated a nap, but one particular sister invited me into the library to talk. She told me she became a sister because of the influence Dr. Cerney had on her life. She told me of the progression of her life since meeting her. I thought that was the end of the conversation, but I could not have been more wrong. She told me stories about Dr. Cerney that I did not want to hear. I was already overwhelmed by knowing too much about her. The last thing I needed was to hear more of the human side of Dr. Cerney. I blocked everything out except for one thing. She said that Dr. Cerney had "loosened her ties to the community." I did not ask what that meant. I had heard enough. I excused myself and went outside. I wandered the grounds of the motherhouse and only returned when it started to rain. The service was about to begin.

The time had come to complete the life of Dr. Cerney, Sister Mary Cerney. The chapel was small and filled quickly with family, friends, and many sisters. I sat to the left of Dr. Cerney's sister-in-law, who made me feel like family. She asked about me and remarked how much I must have cared to have flown all the way from Topeka. The priest guided us through the funeral mass. At the end of the sermon, he invited people to come up to the podium and speak of their relationship with Dr. Cerney. After he said that, I froze for two reasons. Was I once again going to hear more about Dr. Cerney's personal life? Would I have the courage to speak about her impact on me? I was the only patient from Kansas. I felt it was important to say something short. Before I could speak, the priest said there was time for one more person to speak. A woman rose and walked to the podium. I was relieved and disappointed at the same time. Relieved because I didn't know exactly what I was going to say, and I feared I would cry while I was talking. Disappointed because I wanted people to know how, for six years, every day, she sat with me and helped me through depression. I wanted them to know that I became the person I was because of our work together. I was free of medication, navigated my first adult relationship with Kurt, and was very active in the community in Topeka.

The woman talked about their travels around the world and the fun they shared. I was happy to hear this. Dr. Cerney worked hard. She rarely took time away from Menninger.

There was a short break between the talks and the procession to the gravesite. I walked up to the woman who spoke of their travels and said, "I don't know why, but you look familiar. My name is Julie Brown."

Her response shook me. She said loudly, "Oh my God!"

She knew me from one of the times I was a patient at Harding Hospital. She was not one of my treaters, but I knew I'd had some interaction with her. It was clear that she and Dr. Cerney talked about me. *Wow! I was important enough that she talked about our work together*, I thought.

The time came to line up behind the priest, altar boys, and casket. The altar boys carried long gold candle holders. The priest carried a tall gold crucifix. As I stepped out of the chapel into the night, I noticed the weather reflected my mood. It was cold, foggy, and raining slightly. We moved slowly and silently toward her burial spot.

I wasn't sure I would make it through this final goodbye. We stopped about ten feet from the already dug grave, and the priest began to pray. Her casket was hovering over the grave on a graveside stand. As he ended the prayers, I began to feel weak in my knees and was about to hit the ground. A sister standing to my left put her arm around my waist and held me up until I was strong enough to regain my balance.

The service was over in fifteen minutes. As people walked back inside, I lingered. I wanted to see her coffin lowered into her grave. These morbid needs of mine—obsessed with her in her coffin, watching the coffin being lowered—were just that: morbid. I chose to be there. I chose to hear stories about her life. I could have stayed in Topeka and let that be the end. No one else from Topeka was at her final burial. There just seemed no end to this need to be with her until she was buried.

A sister took my hand, guided me away from the burial site, and led me to the dining room for dinner. I was invited to spend the night due to the foggy and rainy evening making driving difficult. I thanked them but had to get away. I had been inundated with sights, sounds, stories, and people. I was overstimulated. The drive back to Columbus would be soothing.

I flew back to Topeka the next day. I felt empty and did not have a plan for how to work through my grief. While on the plane, I read an entry from my diary dated December 2, 1995. Dr. Cerney said, "When a person is in pain, it's hard to focus on anything else." It wasn't a question. It was a statement of how she was feeling.

Chapter Fifteen
MY NEW ANALYST

ONE OF THE FIRST THINGS I did when I returned to Topeka was call Kathleen. I asked her if we could go jogging. She readily agreed. We did not talk much. Halfway through the jog, I stopped and could not breathe. She stood beside me and waited. I was overcome with emotion. She said, "Are you OK? Let's walk the rest of the way."

Her compassion made me cry. We went to a coffee shop and talked about what I might do next. She said she had a friend who was a psychologist and might be able to help me. When we finished talking, I went home and called Kurt. We were not dating at that time, but he came over and soothed me. He sat on the floor with me and listened with great compassion.

I tried to distract myself with work at the Insurance Department by getting there at 6:00 a.m. I put together a case against an insurance agent who was harassing people to buy health insurance. There were calls logged from angry people and formal written complaints against him. By the time people began coming to work, I had the full case ready for the legal division to act. There was not enough to do to keep my mind off my grief.

The weekend after I returned, I lay on my bed sobbing. I needed someone to talk to who could work me through the process of mourning Dr. Cerney's death. I met with two different therapists and one analyst, but no one felt like the right fit. I did not want to go through a whole new psychoanalysis again. I wanted to meet with a specialist in grief therapy for a couple of months and never return to any form of therapy. It was too costly and too painful.

As my crying slowed, it occurred to me that Menninger had a sliding scale clinic for people who could not afford the full cost of psychoanalysis. I called the clinic and was told the director would call me back within two days. I received a call from Dr. Colson. He suggested we meet to discuss my expectations for therapy. I had never worked with a man in psychoanalysis and wasn't sure I could trust a man to grasp the depth of my loss. My father had no capacity for introspection.

Dr. Colson surpassed my expectations. We met on a Thursday at 10:00. He greeted me in the waiting room and led me to his office. He stood about six feet three, was handsome, had pretty gray hair and a slight East Coast twang that I guessed was from growing up in Boston. He was dressed in black pants, a white button-down shirt, and a jacket. His office was very different from Dr. Cerney's. His office was tidy. There were books lining his bookcase in a neat way. There were papers on his desk in orderly piles. The office was larger than Dr. Cerney's, allowing for more space to move around. His chair and the inevitable analytic couch looked comfortable. He gestured for me to sit across from him.

I started by saying, "I doubt you will want to work with me. You will never be able to help me the way Dr. Cerney did. I am angry and I do not want someone to dismiss my anger as transference or any other analytic bullshit. I would understand if you decided not to work with me."

He said nothing for an uncomfortable period of time. He opened with, "I have no intention of taking Dr. Cerney's place. I knew her professionally and we saw each other at social functions. This must be a very confusing time for you."

I was looking for sarcasm, dismissiveness, anything to make me hate him and walk out. I found none of that. He was kind and gentle. He asked many questions. His style was very different from Dr. Cerney's. She was very quiet and said very little. I sensed I could trust him. We agreed to meet again to continue the assessment. I walked out relieved. I thought maybe he could help me understand and unpack this terrible pain.

We decided to meet Monday through Thursday at 12:00. I decided I did not want to go into this relationship not knowing anything about him. I felt burned by not knowing enough about Dr. Cerney until after she died. I went to the Menninger library and began a search for anything he might have written. The library was a reader and researcher's paradise. It was housed in the Tower Building. There was a clock in the middle of the Tower that actually told the correct time. I was self-conscious when I walked through the doors to the library. I thought maybe it was only for professionals. I slid by the front desk and walked straight to the card catalogue to do a literature search. He was published. He had written articles in books and in journals. When I got to the card that identified a journal article dealing with the death of his wife,

I froze. Was I going to learn too much? Was it a boundary issue to read what he had written?

I felt queasy. He discussed the effect on him and studied the effect it had on the work with his patients. It was personal and well-written. He had children. That was important to me. Children meant compassion and patience. I wasn't sure the effect it would have on him if he knew I read the article. I did not tell him for two weeks. The day I decided to tell him I did not lie down on the couch. I sat on the edge and said nothing. He asked me why I didn't feel comfortable lying down.

I said, in carefully measured words, "Two weeks ago I read your article about the death of your wife due to cancer." He said nothing. I could not look at him.

"Why did you wait so long to tell me?" He seemed a little on edge.

"I was scared you would be angry. I was scared because it means you know a lot about losing someone to cancer. I worried it was too hard for you to hear of my grief after Dr. Cerney died. I was just scared."

I heard him let out a slight moan. I became dependent on his almost inaudible moans. When he let out the moan, I felt deep compassion for him, as I think he was feeling for me. I wasn't sure of the content or meaning, but it felt like he was deeply grasping the emotion of the moment.

This was the beginning of a seven-year analytic relationship, a year longer than my relationship with Dr. Cerney. I accomplished a lot during the seven years. I never needed to be on medication, I completed a Master's in Social Work at Washburn University, and was accepted into law school. My relationship with Kurt changed dramatically. Not long after Dr. Cerney died, Kurt and I began dating again. For the first time in my life, I had intercourse. I did not tell Dr. Colson until after it happened. He said, "I thought we were going to talk about this before you did it."

It wasn't actually planned. As with many first sexual relationships, it was spontaneous. I was half awake when it happened and freaked out. I jumped out of bed and kept saying, "Oh my god, oh my god." After that, the "oh my gods" were an expression of great pleasure.

Chapter Sixteen
SOCIAL WORK, LAW SCHOOL, AND SMITH COLLEGE

IN THE EARLY NINETIES, The Menninger Clinic began retiring clinicians because insurance companies were no longer willing to reimburse for long-term inpatient treatment. There were other reasons, but everyone was tight-lipped about why Menninger was slowly closing its doors. The closing of Menninger caused a glut of clinicians in Topeka. The cost of treatment was exorbitant. Dr. Colson opened a private practice in Topeka for a couple years. After a couple years, he decided to move to Kansas City and work as an analyst with a group of other analysts.

I completed my Master's in Social Work while working at the Kansas Insurance Department. I had no intention of practicing as a clinician. My goal was to raise my grade point average enough to be accepted into Washburn Law School. I graduated with a 4.0 GPA and applied to law school the following fall of 2000. I was elated when I received the letter telling me I was accepted. My father, brother, cousins, uncle, and maternal grandfather were all lawyers. The idea of being the first female lawyer in the family propelled me into action. The human resources director at the Insurance Department agreed to pay for half my tuition while I worked part time. My friends were very encouraging. Most of my friends at the department were part of the legal team. They felt I was ready and capable of handling the rigors of classes. I discussed everything with Dr. Colson. We talked about what I might do with a social work and law degree, what type of law might interest me, and how to keep from becoming overwhelmed by the massive amount of information coming my way. I considered becoming a public defender. The combination of social work and the law seemed a perfect match for defending people who could not afford a lawyer.

The books were huge and heavy, literally and figuratively. I went to classes in the morning and worked in the afternoons. There were days I would work three hours in the morning, go to class for three hours, and return to work to finish out the day. I read late into the night about constitutional law, tortes, and criminal law. One morning, I was half listening to the professor speak on a topic about constitutional law that was very technical. He said, "Miss Brown, please stand."

I looked around, hoping there was another Miss Brown in the class. He was looking straight at me. I slowly rose and said nothing. Everyone's heads turned toward me. I began to sweat. I have no idea what he asked me. I stood mute. We stared at each other. The classroom was silent. My mind was completely blank. I actually read what was required for that day, but his words did not compute in my head. He told me to sit down and went on with the class. That was the beginning of the end for me. From that day forward, I was anxious like I never felt since I was discharged from Menninger in 1989. I could not keep up with the daily readings. I could not sleep. Dr. Colson suggested I consult with a psychiatrist and consider medication to relieve the anxiety. I refused. I was not going to let this lead me down the path to depression, mania, and medication.

I decided to spend Thanksgiving with my father and his wife in Key Largo. Before classes broke for the vacation, the same Constitutional Law professor asked us a question that we were to answer when we returned. The question had something to do with protecting wetlands. We were not allowed to use outside resources to research the question. It was to be answered purely by what we were learning in class. One of the first things I did when I got to Key Largo was ask my dad the question.

"Dad, my Constitutional Law professor asked us to answer this question on the wetlands."

I handed him the paper with the question on it. He barely read it and said, "Julie, I don't think law school is a good choice for you. You have been doing so well at the Insurance Department. I would hate to see you jeopardize your job by getting sick again, or quit your job and lose health insurance. You need to be covered by health insurance." This heightened my anxiety. I spent most of my time in the pool overlooking the Atlantic, wondering how to get through what I'd thought was a minor challenge.

I was not doing well when I returned to Topeka. I had trouble eating, focusing, and had very little energy. Depression and anxiety filled my days and nights. Dr. Colson was very concerned and suggested I take a semester off, get recharged, and return in spring. It was all or nothing for me. I was either going to beat this or drop out. I met with Dr. Colson the day after I returned from Key Largo. I was barely able to talk. I did not tell him of my thoughts of dropping out. The next day, before work and before meeting with Dr. Colson, I gathered up my books, took them to the Washburn bookstore, and was refunded most of my money. I then went to the dean and told him of my decision to drop out. We talked about what was causing so much anxiety. He suggested I take a semester off and return after I felt better. I knew I would not return. When I left the dean's office, I immediately felt better. The anxiety and depression slowly lifted. I met with Dr. Colson later that day and told him of my decision. He expressed frustration. He said he wished we had discussed my decision before I acted impulsively. I did not feel I was being impulsive. I knew that if I did not cut and run, I would land in a psychiatric hospital immobilized by depression.

I returned to working full time at the Insurance Department and began considering how to use my master's degree. I was burnt out from working for the state. The work became tedious and insignificant. One morning while reading the paper, I saw a want ad for an outpatient alcohol and drug counselor at a treatment center called Valley Hope. I applied for the position and got it. I was relieved. I was ready to move on to other challenges. Kathleen and her husband Gary threw a going-away party at a restaurant in Topeka. Kathleen said, "Think hard about this decision. You are leaving your good friends. You might miss the convenience of playing golf and tennis with your friends in Topeka."

I said, "I am worried about that too. I know no one in Kansas City, but I have to give this a try. I feel like there is nothing more to accomplish in Topeka. I love that we can play golf on the spur of the moment. I guess we will just have to plan further ahead."

My Analyst's Underwear

I found an apartment in Kansas City and commuted for about six months. My apartment was twenty minutes from Valley Hope in Lee's Summit, Missouri. On my first day, I received a note and flowers from Kathleen. Her support was tremendously important to me. The office never took off. I rarely had individual clients. I met with Dr. Colson at noon and worked from 1:00 p.m. to 9:00 p.m. The majority of my job consisted of running an intensive outpatient program (IOP) three evenings a week on Monday, Wednesday, and Friday. I also ran a group on Tuesdays and Thursdays for patients who completed the IOP and needed continued support.

Kansas City was exciting. The food was good, as was the music. Every Saturday afternoon I went to a bar and listened to Mama Ray belt out blues and jazz. My financial advisor's office was in Kansas City. His wife was part of a tennis group and he hooked me up with them. We played every other weekend. Other than that, I was very alone. I visited friends in Topeka once in a while. Kurt and I were no longer dating. He visited me a couple of times in Kansas City, but that too was a part of my life that was over. I struggled to accept that we would no longer be dating. We talked on the phone and he told me he had a girlfriend. I knew it was over, but he introduced me to so many wonderful people. He was my first adult relationship, leaving me feeling empty without him. I dated men in Kansas City but no one seriously. It did not take me long to figure out that Valley Hope was not where I wanted to be professionally. I felt no sense of accomplishment. I needed something to do that challenged me at a deeper level. The only reason I got my master's degree was to raise my GPA and go to law school. Now that law school was off the table, I decided to investigate the PhD programs that were psychoanalytically focused. I requested an application from Smith College in Northampton, Massachusetts. Their program was respected, and I was told by a student of the program that it was heavy into psychoanalytic clinical training. The program required two years of clinical post-graduate training. I decided to stay with Valley Hope for two years and apply to the PhD program at Smith College.

I completed the clinical work and applied to the Smith College program. Within a month of applying, I received a letter of acceptance. I could barely contain myself. I immediately called my younger sister, Jenny, in Vermont. We talked about how fun it would be to live near each other. She allowed me to send my furniture and various belongings to her house. She said she would hold them until I completed the program. I knew this would work. I would be close to two siblings, Jenny and Will. I loved the East Coast and felt academically prepared for the coursework.

I ended my analysis with Dr. Colson. I have no recollection of how we ended the relationship. I remember standing up and wanting to hug him. He stayed in his seat. I saw tears falling, but I felt unmoved. After seven years of analysis, I walked out of his office, got in my car, and headed to Northampton with a short stop in Columbus. I don't know why I was unable to feel the sadness of ending analysis with Dr. Colson while I was with him. As I drove out of the parking lot, the tears flowed. Endings, since Dr. Cerney died, have been very difficult to share with others.

As the saying goes, hindsight is 20-20. Why did it not occur to me that moving across the country to attend a rigorous PhD program would trigger anxiety and depression? Wasn't it the same as law school? The only difference between the two programs was content. I tanked a month into the program. As depression and anxiety descended, I found it difficult to get to classes. My friends tried to encourage me by sitting with me while studying. My favorite person in the group was a woman who would encourage me to jog with her every morning. I was too ashamed to tell her what I was feeling. At the end of the month, I met with one of my professors. Her office was ridiculously messy. There were books, papers, food, a computer covered with Post-its, and it smelled of coffee and dust, lots of dust. I sat down and told her of my decision to drop out. I could not look at her.

She said, "I knew you would be the first one to drop out."

I said, "Don't try to convince me to stay."

"I won't."

"Where will you go?"

"Columbus."

She let out a disgusted ugh. After she groaned, I left her office, packed up my car, and headed home. I did not ask why she thought I was going to be the first one to drop out. I was too fragile to hear what might have been critical. I made the trip home in one day.

Chapter Seventeen
RETURN TO THE SCENE OF THE CRIME

I SPENT A SIGNIFICANT amount of money on tuition when I went to law school. I was getting low on resources. When I worked full time for Valley Hope, I built up my reserves. After quitting the job at Valley Hope and starting the PhD program at Smith, I knew I would need more money to complete the program, but I dropped out before needing the money. The Christmas after I dropped out of Smith College, my dad gifted the four of us a significant amount of money. When I opened the envelope and saw the check, my mind went blank. All of my siblings were laughing out of joy and thanking my dad. I sat on the chair and said nothing. I could not believe my eyes. My dad walked over to me and said, "Julie, what's wrong?" He laughed and said something like, "Is it not enough?"

"Of course that's not it. I keep thinking of the bible story where a father gave his three sons money and one buried it, one invested it, and the other spent it on lavish parties. I'm not sure what to do with this amount of money."

He said, "Do not touch the principal. Just use the dividends."

I was naive about money and didn't even understand what that meant. My father invited his financial advisor to our house that day. He answered all of our questions. The financial advisor suggested we not pay too much attention to the day-to-day amount of the stock because this was money for the future. He said the stock market rises and falls and to review the monthly statements.

This money did not take away the severe depression and anxiety I was feeling when I returned home from Smith. I knew I needed a job, but I wasn't sure how I could hold one with the intensity of my emotional breakdown. I had to take a test that would allow me to practice social work in Ohio. I hated tests. I went into the testing center wondering if depression would keep me from passing it. I had to answer 80 percent of the questions correctly, and that is exactly what I did.

I was living in my sister Kimberlee's basement, looking for a place to live and a place to work. Every part of my body hurt. Depression is not just mental, it is physical. Getting up, showering, and eating took immense energy. I also needed to find a therapist. I started with getting a job. I got a job at Netcare. It was a 24-hour psychiatric crisis facility for people who needed support for the night or had to be hospitalized. The clientele were either homeless or poor. I assessed each person and either had them hospitalized or scheduled them an appointment with a mental health outpatient facility. The assessments took two hours. There were days when in between assessments I would lay on the floor of my office in a fetal position and close my eyes. Depression was taking a terrible toll on me. When I went home, I usually ate very little and lay in bed for twelve hours.

A month after returning home, I was on my way out of a movie theater and I ran into a high school friend. We talked about what we were doing in life and I said, "Where are you living?"

Terry said "I'm living in my brother's basement."

"That's amazing! I'm living in Kimberlee's basement."

We exchanged phone numbers. He said, "You will never call me."

"Why not?"

He said, "Just an instinct."

A week later I called him and asked if he thought we might make good roommates. I needed to get out of Kimberlee's basement soon. Life was feeling a little tense in their home. Terry definitely needed to move because he was commuting a half hour or more to his painting jobs. I wanted to live in or near Bexley, a suburb of Columbus. He and I both grew up in the area. His mom lived in Bexley, and he liked to check up on her frequently.

I found an apartment in one day. I called Terry and asked him to check it out. He loved it and the moving process began. I had nothing but clothes and furniture given to me by Kevin and Kimberlee. Terry also had very little. Terry was the best person I could have lived with. He was funny, laid back, and did not judge me for being depressed. On the weekends, when I wasn't working, he would grab me and drag me to Graeter's for ice cream.

I did not last a year at Netcare. Depression and anxiety were preventing me from sustaining any level of competency at work. My next step was to find a therapist and psychiatrist. Kimberlee was working as a therapist at an outpatient clinic called the Gestalt Institute. Gestalt therapy and psychoanalysis were two very different forms of treatment. Gestalt worked in the here and now. Intense emotional exchanges between therapist and client were the cornerstones of Gestalt therapy. This was clearly very different than lying on the couch, not looking at the therapist, and saying what came to mind without a filter. Kimberlee talked to the owner of the institute about my condition. He suggested I meet with his most seasoned therapist, Beth, and if necessary, meet with their psychiatrist.

I dragged myself to the Institute, found the waiting room closest to her office, and collapsed on the couch. I closed my eyes and wondered how anyone could help me. I had been through thirteen years of psychoanalysis, living the best times of my life, and here I was, back to the scene of the crime, as sick as I was when I left Columbus in 1988. I felt devastated and defeated.

I did not hear her come out of her office. "Julie?"

I opened my eyes, said nothing. Beth was standing about five feet from me. She said nothing else. I slowly rose and followed her into her office. It was huge. There was a very long couch with a blanket and tissue box sitting at the corner of the couch; her desk, computer, other chairs around the room; plants, a bookcase, and lots of windows. I noticed bushes and trees surrounding the windows. The lighting was soft. I wasn't sure where to sit, so she motioned me to the couch and pulled a chair in front of me. I thought, *Now this is different. A therapist, sitting in front of me, looking directly at me?* I could not look at her. We sat quietly for a couple minutes.

"How are you doing?"

I lifted my gaze and saw a woman in her early fifties, dressed professionally in what she would later call her uniform—black or brown pants, color-coordinated shoes, and a blouse or sweater that matched. She wore earrings and a wedding band. If she was wearing makeup, it was not noticeable. Her eyes were blue, and her hair was of medium length. She sat squarely in her chair, feet grounded.

While I was making my observations she said, "Is the couch comfortable?"

"Yes."

I did not want her to suggest that I lie down on the couch like I did in psychoanalysis. Even though I could barely make eye contact, I needed someone to be present with me by looking at me.

There was a long pause. The pauses felt respectful. If she had jumped in and pelted me with questions, I don't think I would have returned. For fifty minutes, Beth and I talked about how hard I was struggling with depression and anxiety. At times, I would lay my head on the back of the couch, close my eyes and answer her questions. I was exhausted. She asked if I had been on medication in the past.

I said, "I have been on many medications that never came close to relieving depression. I was discharged from the Menninger Clinic in 1989 and never needed medication. I really hate the thought of going through the long process of finding the right medication."

"I understand. Do you want to meet again before we talk about medication?"

"No. I need something because I don't know how much longer I can feel like this."

"Do you feel like hurting yourself?"

"I have no plan. I just have fleeting thoughts."

"If you did feel like hurting yourself, would you tell me?"

I responded yes.

By the end of the session, I felt a bit better. I could tell she and I would work well together. The pace of her questions and her comfort with silence gave me the confidence to commit to return. The types of questions she asked and her affect relayed warmth and genuine concern. She said she would talk to the psychiatrist and call me back with times he would be available to meet for an assessment.

Within three days, I received a call directly from the psychiatrist. His name was Dr. Raymond W. Waggoner, Jr. We met the following Tuesday. Once more, I dragged myself to the institute and collapsed on the couch in his waiting room. At exactly 1:00, Dr. Waggoner walked around the corner and introduced himself. Intuition is very important to me and I have learned to trust it. I felt confident that he could help me the minute I met him. I sat in a chair that was near the couch. His office was a little smaller than Beth's. His desk was stacked with files, papers, and books. There were toys in the corners of his office. I later learned he was also a child psychiatrist. I was no less depressed that day than I was when I met with Beth. I answered his questions with very few words. I had no energy to fill in too many details. He seemed unaffected by my short answers. He never pressured me for more information. He was very kind and gentle in how he asked questions. He had piercing but not threatening eyes. We met for an hour.

He said, "Well, Julie, I think you need to be on an anti-depressant. You told me you have been manic in the past. I would like you to try Effexor. There is a risk that comes with this medication for people who have had a manic episode. Effexor could trigger mania."

"I don't care. I choose mania over this hell."

Within weeks, depression turned into mania. My work with Beth changed dramatically. I could not stop talking. I had pressured speech, meaning one sentence rolled into the next with no apparent connection. I brought in music and made her listen to seven songs from seven different CDs. When manic, I spend lots of money. I called my broker to make sure I could pay for everything by check. I bought a new Harley Davidson motorcycle. There were chaps, steel-toed boots, a leather jacket embossed with the Harley Davidson name on the back, two helmets, two pairs of gloves, and two pairs of goggles. I had the seat changed to one that would fit two people. No one ever rode with me, but I needed to be prepared. I stopped sleeping and felt exhilarated. I became psychotic and thought I could read people's minds. I became paranoid and knew the secret service was following me around Columbus. I made new friends and found synchronicity in everything. The synchronicity expressed itself in an exchange I had with a woman at Starbucks. I was standing in line and said, "You look lovely. Have we met before?"

"I don't know. I am an administrator at the Minster School." I had never heard of it.

We talked further and she invited me to visit the school. I met her there after we got our coffee.

"This school is for underprivileged children. We get grants that help pay their tuition. We are currently running a fundraiser."

Before I thought it through, I whipped out my checkbook and wrote the school a check for one thousand dollars. Impulsivity guided my behavior. What I have just described is the classic definition of a manic episode. The challenging part for people to understand when I am manic is that behavior like this is a symptom.

I began talking about riding my motorcycle to Topeka to visit friends I had not seen since 2002. Someone in the family took my motorcycle keys away for fear I would hurt myself. Dr. Waggoner and Beth decided it was time to have a family meeting. My life was spinning out of control. In the meantime, Dr. Waggoner prescribed Lithium. It may have worked, but goiters developed on my thyroid. The only treatment was to stop taking Lithium.

We met as a family at the Gestalt Institute with the owner of the institute running the meeting. Will and Jenny were brought into the meeting through speakerphone.

The owner said, "Julie has done some dangerous and terrible things."

I said, "Takes one to know one." I could not keep my mouth shut.

The end result of the meeting was that I canceled my trip to Topeka, the motorcycle keys stayed with a family member, and discussion began about hospitalization.

It was 2005 and I had not been hospitalized since my discharge from Menninger in 1989. My roommate, Terry, drove me to Mount Carmel West. I was assessed and admitted quickly. The psychiatrist was excellent. He was one of the few psychiatrists who actually looked at me while we were talking. I felt like he cared. I don't know what medication he prescribed, but I slowly came down from the high. Dr. Waggoner visited me. I would barely let him get in a word. During an activity, I made him a bracelet out of beads and spelled out the word "soul" at each end of the bracelet. When I gave it to him he said, "There are two souls spelled out on the bracelet."

"I know! Do you get it? Do you get it? We are two souls passing through this world together."

He lowered his head and took a hard gulp. I think he was moved by the gesture. Visiting hours were up and we rose. I said, "I'm not going to hug you because I don't want anyone to think I like you too much." He chuckled.

Five days before I was discharged, I was sitting in a chair facing a window watching snow fall onto the street below, lit up by a streetlamp. A patient walked toward me, put a chair in front of me, and began rubbing my feet. He said nothing. I did not feel threatened. "How long have you been here?" I asked.

"A month. I will be discharged tomorrow."

"Where will you go?"

"Nowhere. I am homeless."

It was a frigid winter and I asked if he had socks and gloves and a heavy coat. He said he had one pair of socks and no gloves and a coat. He told me he was a veteran, and due to depression he could not pull his life together. He returned to his room, leaving me thinking and scared for him. I had three pairs of socks and two pairs of gloves. In the morning I asked my psychiatrist if I could give him my gloves and socks. The psychiatrist said it might not be a good idea to get involved. He said the hospital had extra clothes for people and that he would take care of him. That was the last time I saw the patient. This was not the last time I was a patient at Mount Carmel West due to mania.

Chapter Eighteen
THE MEN'S PRISON

I HELD SEVEN JOBS from the time I returned from Smith College in 2002 to 2010. I either quit because I was bored or was drinking on the job.

I believe I begin drinking when my medications are no longer working. I do not deny that I am an alcoholic. I have attended self-help groups in the past. However, Beth pointed out that I have never used the meetings to help me stay sober. She is correct. I use meetings to meet people and become less isolated.

While looking for a job on the internet, I noticed an ad for a social worker to work at a men's prison in London, Ohio. This type of job was not exactly an experience I was prepared for after graduating from the Columbus School for Girls. London was a forty-minute drive from Columbus. It was a contract job, meaning I would not be working for the state. I would be eligible to work for the state after a probationary period. The contractor did a background check, interviewed me, and quickly hired me. The pay was $20 an hour. That was the most I had ever made working.

I spent the first two weeks in orientation with a man who did more talking about his life and how much beer he drank every night than about training. I assumed all of my training would occur on the job. I followed a social worker around for a week and then I was on my own.

The prison held approximately 2,500 men in various levels of security. The levels ranged from medium to super max. The first day on the job excited me. I probably should have felt fear, but it didn't enter my mind. The day began by walking through a security check. I handed my backpack to a guard. He or she would go through my bag making sure there were no drugs, glass, weapons, or anything they might feel was some form of contraband. After being cleared, I went through a heavy metal door that opened up into the yard. The yard was bigger than I expected. I saw men playing basketball, smoking, sitting on bleachers talking, and jogging or walking around the edges of the yard. My office was a converted cell. The cinder block walls, no window, and metal door that I never closed reminded me where I was. I was locked in a prison, surrounded by men who committed crimes, some murder.

I walked to the captain's office to get a list of prisoners who were placed in isolation due to not obeying various rules in the prison—anything from fighting to not obeying an order.

"Good Morning, Captain. How many inmates messed up yesterday after I left?"

He joked and said, "Yeah, it's your fault for leaving, Julie. They always mess up after you leave."

After obtaining the list, I headed to my office, flipped on the computer, and made a list of what to do that day. My job was regimented. My duties were done at the same time every day. The first interaction I had with prisoners for the day was visiting inmates in isolation. I liked getting that out of the way due to its medieval feel—an outdated way of treating a human being.

I always moved slowly while in the yard. While I was not scared, I was not stupid. There were not too many women who worked inside the yard. I was cautious. I made sure I knew where the guards were standing.

Standing at the entrance to the isolation building, I was buzzed in. The smell of stink hit me like a ton of bricks. It was a mix of sweat, urine, and stale food. I was greeted with a nod, but pretty much ignored. A typical interaction with an inmate in isolation was a knock on the metal door and then peering through the small opening. I could see a bed but not much else. I knew there was a head and barely enough room to walk around. I would say the inmate's name and usually get no response.

"Just checking to see how you are doing. If you need to talk or need anything else let me know."

Silence.

On one rare occasion, a prisoner asked for a book. I thought that was a good sign. He was in isolation for twenty-three hours with one hour outside in a caged area. Reading, while difficult due to little lighting, meant he wanted to be taken out of his head and maybe escape to a better place. After finding a paperback in the prison library, I handed it to him. As I was about to walk out, a guard said, "I wouldn't get in the habit of doing that."

"Doing what?"

"Giving a prisoner a book. They have been known to eat the pages to get out of isolation and taken to the infirmary."

Eat a book? That confirmed the inhumanity of isolation.

The rest of my day was filled with visiting prisoners in their dorms after being released from a cell specifically designed for prisoners who had expressed suicidality, meeting prisoners with a diagnosed mental illness, or just completing paperwork to put in their files. While I said I was not scared in the yard, I was scared of two things. Almost every day, I met in a small room filled with new prisoners. There was always a guard wandering the hall outside the room, but the door was shut. If a surly new prisoner decided to try to get out, I was the first person in his way. This process was called orientation. I told them what to expect, told them to advise me if they needed to talk, and then they filled out a questionnaire. I don't recall what the questionnaire was about, but I do remember only handing them blunted pencils. Blunting a newly sharpened pencil could prove challenging without breaking the tip off and needing to start over again.

The second most scary part of my job was meeting with prisoners in my office who had a mental illness. My office chair sat to the right of the open door about five feet from the prisoner. The prisoner's chair sat next to the door, blocking my exit. I could think of no other way to position myself to feel safe. It would have taken one short step and I would be history. There was one particular inmate who instilled fear in me the first time I met with him. He stood about six feet, four inches tall, and he weighed over 200 pounds. He sat down and said nothing. I waited him out.

"What do you know about being in a prison for life?" he asked.

Great question. I knew exactly nothing. I did not answer right away because my brain froze. After about three minutes I said, "Only what you tell me."

That appeared to be the right answer. From that point on, he opened up about his day-to-day life. He told me he was bored most of the time, hated the food, and kept to himself to avoid getting into fights. I never asked an inmate what he did to end up incarcerated. However, this prisoner told me he committed murder. When I am nervous, I hum a soothing song. With this prisoner, I began humming "The Star-Spangled Banner" low enough that he could not hear me.

One afternoon, after completing my work, I was tired and needed to rest. My desk was large and had an overhang that faced the back of the office. I walked around the desk, rolled under it, and took a snooze. I left my door slightly open. A couple minutes after lying down, I heard the creak of the door open and heard one of my supervisors say, "No, she's not here. No, I looked everywhere."

I didn't know what to do. As quickly as he walked in, he walked out. I lay there for a couple minutes, trying to come up with a plan. How soon should I walk out of my office? How long should I lay there? After ten minutes, I rolled out from under the desk and began making noises. I coughed and moved around the office so people could hear me. I grabbed my backpack and quickly left the building. No one asked where I was, but I knew the end of this job was coming. The boredom and monotony were wearing me down. Another job down the tank.

Chapter Nineteen
HOSPITALIZATION 15

IN JANUARY 2013, I became severely depressed and quickly flipped to mania. This was the worst episode I ever experienced. I was paranoid and hallucinating. I thought people were trying to kill me. I also thought people were trying to protect me from the people who were trying to kill me. I went on another buying spree. Ten thousand dollars later and I had new clothes and shoes I did not need. I bought a coat from Nordstrom for over $700.

    I was too paranoid to stay in my apartment, so I packed a bag and checked into the Hilton at Easton. Easton is an upscale shopping area with great restaurants. Three nights after I checked in, President Obama was giving the State of the Union address. I became obsessed with my friend Kathleen Sebelius and her tenure as Secretary of Health and Human Resources due to glitches in the Affordable Care Act. A month before, I saw her grilled by a senate committee, and she was tense in a way I had never seen her. The night of the address, I was talking to Beth and she was scared. She knew I was manic and wanted me to get to a hospital as quickly as possible. I told her I would check in after I saw Kathleen on TV. I knew from previous speeches that the camera would show cabinet members as they walked into the chamber. The minute I saw her, I relaxed and saw that she was OK. She was smiling and I felt she was holding her own.

Beth said, "I want you to go to the hospital and convince them you are manic."

That wasn't hard to do. I talked non-stop. I drove to Riverside Hospital and was quickly admitted. Every time the security guard walked by my room, I ran to the back because I thought he would try to hurt me. I believed I was the second coming of Christ. The staff were overwhelmed by my hyperactivity.

"Julie, stay in your room."

I stood right at the edge and said, "Is this OK or would you like me to step back?"

"Just stay behind the line and try to keep your voice down."

At one point I felt I was being mistreated and asked to speak to the director of the hospital.

I become very entitled and arrogant when I am manic. I did not sit or lie down for twenty-four hours. I was hungry and thirsty. The room was really cold, and I wouldn't wear the hospital-issue slippers.

The next evening, Beth visited me. I said, "I am so angry at you! I want you to take your shoes and socks off and feel how cold this floor is!"

I was sobbing. She quietly and calmly listened to me, but there was nothing she could do at this point. I was being held on a pink slip. This meant the hospital could keep me for seventy-two hours to be assessed as to whether I was a danger to myself or others. I remember nothing about what we talked about in the assessment.

The hospital social worker said, "Where would you like to be treated? We have a bed here, but it's your choice."

I thought for a moment and said, "I want to be transferred to Netcare."

I figured since I worked there before, they would give me medication and discharge me. I felt safe there. I was taken by ambulance to Netcare. I showered, had something to eat, and fell asleep.

Early the next morning, a psychiatrist sat in a chair outside my room and within four minutes said, "Manic." He wrote orders for me to be pink-slipped to the state hospital, Twin Valley Behavioral Healthcare.

Losing all rights is a disorienting and scary thing. I could make phone calls, but I was so confused that I could not remember anybody's phone number. My family had no idea where I was. Dr. Waggoner and Beth called my sister Kim and updated her on my grave condition. I ate nothing for a long time because I thought the food was poisoned.

Chapter Twenty
DESCENT INTO HELL

I TOOK ANOTHER AMBULANCE RIDE, except this one was to the state hospital. I was wearing two hospital gowns and nothing on my feet. The EMTs covered me with a blanket. It was the first week of January 2013. I was deposited at the state hospital and waited for staff to admit me. It took forty-five minutes and I paced the admission area. I was embarrassed standing in the intake area with a flimsy hospital gown and nothing on my feet. The intake area was cold, and I wanted to put on my street clothes. The only clothes I had were what I wore to Riverside Hospital. When intake was complete, staff allowed me to put my clothes on. A staff member escorted me to the ward. As I walked in, I heard a loud bang. I was locked in for the next thirteen days.

There were patients milling around the dayroom. The room was cold and had a sour smell. I noticed there were more men than women. I was not scared of the patients; I was scared of the staff. It seemed as if no one wanted to work with any of us. After so many hospitalizations, I knew the staff had control over everything we did. I was still so paranoid that I thought the state police were going to storm the hospital and break me out.

I had only the clothes on my back and I wore them for thirteen days. There were washers and dryers that I used infrequently. I was escorted to my room. It was very depressing. There were two small beds, a window, and a bathroom. I couldn't see them, but there were cameras everywhere watching our every move.

One day when I walked out of the room, a psych tech was walking toward me wearing a T-shirt that said *Brilliant*.

I said, "Are you?"

"Am I what?"

"Brilliant?"

"No, but I know a lot!"

The man with the "brilliant" T-shirt (his name was Terrence) and a tech named Gloria made us feel that they genuinely cared about our treatment. They mingled with us on the ward and thought of ways to keep us occupied. It was a cold winter, so we were rarely let out onto the enclosed patio. However, one afternoon, Terrence broke ranks and let us out onto the snow-covered patio.

He said, "I bet no one can lob a snowball over the wall."

Three of us took the challenge. We were having fun until one of the nurses came out and corralled us inside. It was the last taste of fresh air I got for a long time.

My memory is hazy, but I do not remember meeting with my social worker or psychiatrist for days. As a social worker, I knew the policy was to meet with the patient within twenty-four hours of being admitted and develop a treatment plan. With nothing better to do, I paced the halls. I was achy for exercise. The halls were pale white and depressed me. A typical day went this way: Breakfast arrived at 7:00 a.m. A staff member would yell out our last names, and when the patient stepped forward, he or she was handed a tray. When my name was called, I felt like a cow being called in to eat. The food was horrible. Food was used as a bargaining tool. "Does anyone want to trade their mashed potatoes for bread?"

There were patients walking around holding their pants up from losing so much weight. After eating, the day was long and grueling. I read the paper and watched the news. The TV was only allowed on when there were no activities. I attended one activity in the two weeks I was there. We used popsicle sticks to make a box that was stuck together with Elmer's Glue. One day I had a full-time job, the next day I was playing with popsicle sticks.

On one rare occasion, my psychiatrist asked to meet with me. She said, "You are pregnant."

"That's impossible. I haven't had sex in years," I said.

"Are you sure?"

They checked the test again and got a false positive. I was so paranoid that I thought they thought one of the techs had raped me and they were checking to see if I would do anything about it if I was told I was pregnant. The only barrier between the men's bedroom and women's bedroom was a person who was supposed to be sitting in a chair at the far end of the hall. I never once saw anyone sitting in the chair.

One of the techs said to me, "If you knew what that patient did to women, the hair on the back of your neck would rise. Keep your distance from him."

That's the kind of environment in which we were supposed to

heal. One day a man was being admitted, and in the process, he yelled that he would rather go back to jail. It was more than scary on the unit. I was so scared of being in my bedroom that I began sleeping on the floor by the entrance to the unit. For about four nights, I would put a pillow and blanket on the floor and cower there until morning. Every night I did that, the techs and nurse would slam the heavy metal door to the nurse's station in an attempt to make me move back to my room. The sound was deafening and kept me awake all night.

I always took my evening medications at 10:00 p.m. The pills came in a plastic cup. I was handed the cup with fully formed pills and water. The nurse made sure I swallowed them, and I went to bed. One night, the plastic cup was filled with what looked like white dust. I looked up at the nurse and said, "Why are my pills crumbled up?"

"Oh, they come that way sometimes out of the package."

Less than half an hour later I began feeling nauseous and light-headed. I dragged myself to the nurse's station and told the nurse I was not feeling well. He took my blood pressure. I don't remember what it was, but it was so low that the nurse commented he was surprised I hadn't fainted. He told me to go back to my room and he would talk to me. His advice was to drink more water. This reaction from taking my medication never occurred before. I cannot prove this, but I think they were either trying to make me very sick because I was such a pain in the ass, or they tried to kill me.

The next morning, I told one of the techs what happened, and he said that there was a cemetery on grounds. I knew it was time to get the hell out. I requested to be released that day.

My psychiatrist decided to probate me. This meant that I had to meet with an independent psychiatrist who would assess my condition and decide if I needed to continue to be hospitalized. I also met with a public defender. He too assessed my mental capacity. The public defender decided I no longer needed hospitalization and said he would file the paperwork at the end of the day, and I would be released the next day. I begged him twice to remember to file the paperwork. He did not.

The next morning, I was sitting in the dayroom wondering what I would do when I was discharged, when I was told to go to court. I said, "I don't have to go to court. The paperwork has been filed. I am being discharged today."

Terrence said, "Go to court."

I was escorted to a room within the hospital that was set up like a courtroom. When I walked in, there were about fifteen people sitting behind me observing the process. They were students and interns learning about probate court. My public defender guided me to a table, and we sat down. I asked him why I had to go to court since he'd said I would be discharged after he filed the paperwork. He said he forgot to file the paperwork but had full confidence I would be discharged. I had very little confidence in what he said. The prosecutor was sitting at a table to our left. The judge was sitting at the front of the room. The independent psychiatrist was called to the stand and asked by the judge if he felt I needed continued hospitalization. The psychiatrist said, "No. She does not meet probate criteria and should be discharged by the end of the day."

Did I hear him right? Discharged by the end of the day? I was sure the prosecutor would intervene and provide evidence why I should not be discharged. The judge turned to me and said, "You are free to leave the hospital. Take your medication."

The public defender asked that my case be expunged, and the judge agreed. That was it. The hell was over. Within hours I would be discharged. When I walked back to the ward, my psychiatrist asked what happened. I told her I did not meet criteria to continue to be held and should be discharged that afternoon. I was ecstatic! I called my sister Kimberlee who agreed to pick me up around 3:00.

My car was at Riverside Hospital where I was first assessed thirteen days ago. My sister dropped me off at my car. I was a little nervous. I was also still a bit hypomanic. The first thing I did was look for a pack of cigarettes I'd left in the car, found the lighter, and lit up. Smoking never felt so good. It was a beautiful winter day. I took the long way home and just enjoyed being out in the world again.

That was six years ago. It was not long after I was discharged from the state hospital that I began to consider writing this book. I didn't get a job for a while and needed something to fill my time. I also felt I had something to say about the mental health system. My experience at the state hospital, Twin Valley Behavioral Healthcare, reminded me of a modern-day version of *One Flew Over the Cuckoo's Nest*. The incompetence was astounding. Attempting to heal in a place like that is impossible. I found out that the patients had to wait until their symptoms passed and then they might be discharged. I worried for those patients who had symptoms that did not get better. It was actually quite hard to leave my fellow inmates behind. I still wonder where they are and what they are doing.

Chapter Twenty-One
THE NOW

MY LIFE TODAY IS FAIRLY SIMPLE. I walk Micki two miles in the morning. Sometimes I take her to the dog park and let her run off-leash. Nothing pleases me more than to see her run, jump, and play with the other dogs. I go to the YMCA and spin, swim, and attend yoga classes. I see the same people there every morning and enjoy the companionship. I haven't been in such good shape since I lived in Topeka. I take medication in the morning and at night. I grocery shop for my mom and take her to doctor appointments. I visit my sister Kimberlee and her children frequently, but as they enter their teen years, I see them less.

About three years ago I had a job that I loved but lost it. The day I lost the job, I was sitting in my car talking to Beth and sobbing. That was when the perseveration began. There is a special place in hell for the symptom of perseveration. For the past three years, from the moment I wake up until I go to bed, I have to fight saying the same phrases over and over again in my head. Sometimes the thoughts have to be in alphabetical order. Some of the phrases make no sense. Beth and Dr. Waggoner have been trying to help me stop perseverating. A specialist in Mason, Ohio, suggested taking Tramadol. It worked for a couple months, but a side effect forced me to discontinue its use. He also suggested taking a food supplement. Unfortunately, that did not work. I tried cannabinoid oil but felt no relief. I am currently taking Ativan and Lamictal in the morning and Seroquel at night. Those medications seem to take the edge off. Two ways I fight the onslaught of thoughts are to listen to the radio non-stop and sing the same song throughout the day. Yoga, spinning, swimming, and meditation are also helpful.

Most recently, Beth and I came up with the idea that when I was fired, my ego took a hit. My sense of self became confused. I do not yet understand how or why this happened. Something very frightening happened during that job and its ending that caused me to perseverate. We think the perseveration is protecting me from something painful that I have yet to address in therapy. After so many years in therapy, I find it hard to believe there is something still hidden from my consciousness that causes pain. I have complete confidence that this symptom will abate. Deep therapy, the right medication, exercise, and eating healthy are the keys to my sustained sanity.

I would like to leave the reader with one thought. I am who I am because of bipolar disorder, not in spite of bipolar disorder. By that I mean, while bipolar disorder can be life threatening, I am more whole as a result of the outstanding treatment I have received from Dr. Waggoner, Beth, and other past treaters. The analogy I use to describe mental illness to those who can't or won't grasp it, is to compare it to a person who has to go to kidney dialysis every day or every week. The treatment is life-saving. So too is treatment for mental illness. Mental illness is a brain disease and requires diligence through psychotherapy, medication, and exercise. If you suffer bipolar disorder, a mood disorder, or any other mental illness and have not died, you are doing something very right. Healing is about progress, not perfection.

If I Can Stop One Heart from Breaking

If I can stop one heart from breaking,
I shall not live in vain.
If I can ease one life the aching,
Or cool one pain,
Or help one fainting robin,
I shall not live in vain.

—Emily Dickinson

ADDENDUM

I REACHED AN ALL-TIME HIGH. On March 31, 2019, I was hospitalized for the seventeenth time. I beat the all-time high. I sought psychiatric care at an East Coast hospital.

I had not slept for three days and the perseveration was unstoppable. My older brother agreed to care for Micki. I packed a bag full of the basics needed when in a psychiatric hospital: shoes without laces, boxer shorts to sleep in with an oversized T-shirt, one pair of corduroys, a crossword puzzle book, and a fleece jacket. I drove to the Mount Carmel East ER and was admitted. I told the intake staff I was not suicidal but hopeless, and I did not want to get to the point of feeling suicidal. A lovely woman named Christina took care of me while I waited for the social worker to find a bed. They treated me as suicidal because I told them I was hopeless. Everything was taken from me except my crossword puzzle book. I put on a hospital gown and waited. While waiting to be transported by ambulance to the psychiatric hospital, I watched one of my favorite movies twice—*Law Abiding Citizen*.

Twelve hours later, I was transported to Columbus Springs East. I did not know I could drive directly to Columbus Springs East and be admitted, or I would have taken myself there. I was cold, hungry, exhausted. It was about 3:00 a.m. I filled out the required paperwork and was guided to the unit. The staff were wonderful. One thing I never experienced in my previous hospitalizations was stripping to my underwear. At Columbus Springs East they observed if I had bruises so as not to be sued if I had been beaten. The only thing missing was to bend over and cough.

I paced for hours, waiting for the psychiatrist to meet with me. He appeared on the unit at 6:30 a.m. and met with me within an hour. I was so glad we met early because the pacing was wearing me out. We met for over an hour. He amazed me with his thoroughness, and quickly began prescribing medications. He was a slight man in stature, Pakistani, humble and kind. I referred to him as a Pakistani version of Dr. Waggoner. After we met, I went to my room and tried to rest, but I couldn't last longer than ten minutes in bed. The pacing continued.

One morning, three days into my stay at the hospital, I decided to engage an elderly black man. He always sat in the same chair with his chin in his hand and looked very depressed. I asked him where he was from.

He said, "West Virginia."

I asked how he ended up in Columbus.

"Well, Cleveland was dirty, I couldn't spell Cincinnati, so I moved to Columbus."

That really cracked me up. He was always throwing out funny barbs. He said he did not want to become a coal miner. He retired as a custodian after thirty years. I can only imagine he was a favorite of the kids in the school where he worked.

Other patients slowly awoke. We moved as a group to the dining room for breakfast. The meals were sufficient. There were two staff members with us every time we went to the dining room or outside. We were allowed outside four times a day. I never missed a chance to go outside. The routine was fairly similar every day. Meals, meet with the psychiatrist, activities, and lots of down time, at least for me. I went to two activities. After being put on new medications, I was very sleepy and could not make it through an activity. I was not there to attend music therapy or any other group activity. I was there to be properly medicated and find a good psychiatrist I could meet with on an outpatient basis. Before hospitalization I was meeting with a nurse practitioner, but I needed inpatient help. Thankfully, the psychiatrist was willing and able to see me on an outpatient basis. I was thrilled.

The insomnia continued for two more days. The psychiatrist continued to change my medications. After three days, I slept four hours. It felt like I just took a vacation by the ocean. The next day I slept six hours. I knew he got it right—and in such a short period of time. I now tell my family and friends I am on enough medication to kill a horse, but follow that up with, "I don't care because it is helping."

I was discharged Monday, April 8. The staff moved fast getting me discharged. The paperwork was voluminous. The hospital paid

Uber to take me to my car back at Mount Carmel East where I'd left it. I was surprised I could find it. I decided to spend the night at my older sister Kim's home. The thought of returning to my empty apartment after living with so many people felt lonely. I picked Micki up the next morning and I took her straight to the dog park. The freedom I felt was intensely emotional. The perseveration was at a minimum and I was sleeping.

The last time I met with Dr. Waggoner at the end of November 2018, he told me I could call him and update him on my progress. I called him the day I was discharged and explained my experience at Columbus Springs East. I said, "I really like the psychiatrist. Not as much as you."

He said, "That's OK."

I told him all the medications I was on and how good I felt.

In the way that only he says things, he said, "Take off and fly!" It made me tear up. My therapist, Beth, and I continue meeting once a week. However, with the amount of medications I am on, it is hard to dig deep. We'll get there.

ACKNOWLEDGMENTS

HOW CAN I POSSIBLY THANK the many people who supported me and encouraged me to keep going? These individuals include psychiatrists, psychologists, social workers, activities therapists, nurses, psych techs, cleaning staff, family, and teachers. My friends at the Eldon and Elsie Ward YMCA, where I work out, have provided me with friendship and the motivation to suit up and show up. The Y has been my second home for many years. The help everyone has provided me is beyond measure. With seventeen hospitalizations under my belt, I know I will leave someone out. Therefore, I will focus on three people and my dog.

I have known Mo for forty-one years. She is a spiritual director and defines the word "devoted." She is devoted to her husband, three children, their spouses, and seven grandchildren. My thoughts go to one of Celine Dion's songs:

"You were my strength when I was weak, you were my voice

when I couldn't speak, you were my eyes when I couldn't see, you saw the best there was in me, you stood by me and I stood tall, I had your love I had it all… I thank you for each day you gave me… I was blessed because I was loved by you."

This song captures Mo beautifully.

With complete love in my heart, I call my psychiatrist, Dr. Raymond Waggoner, Saint Raymond. I have never met anyone like him. His ability to find the right medication for me is just short of miraculous. We have worked together for fourteen years. He has been there when I was depressed and manic. He visited me in the hospital on more than one occasion. He has a grin that makes me smile. Awhile back, I did not have a car and decided to walk to my appointment with him. I gave myself ninety minutes. An hour into the walk, I realized I was going to be late. I called his office and told his assistant where I was and asked if I should turn around and reschedule. She said she would tell Dr. Waggoner where I was. I decided to keep trudging along. Ten minutes later, a car pulled over and I thought how nice it was that someone was going to give me a ride. That someone was Dr. Waggoner. This story expresses the beauty of this man.

Dr. Waggoner called me recently and said he decided to retire at the end of December 2018. I could barely speak when he told me of his decision to retire. He has certainly earned it, but it breaks my heart. It is shocking how fast fourteen years goes by.

When I returned from Smith College fourteen years ago, I was clinically depressed. The owner of the Gestalt Institute referred me to Beth, one of his seasoned clinicians. I remember my first session with her. I was sitting in the waiting room with my head against the back of the couch. My eyes were closed. I wondered how anybody could help me. The depression was so deep that I could hardly move. I heard my name, opened my eyes, and saw Beth standing in front of me. She invited me into her office and placed a chair in front of me. I was sitting on her couch. I sensed that she was going to be able to help me. Her confidence, warm smile, and laid back manner spoke to me. She spent many hours with me even when I could barely speak. I sometimes wish I stayed in Topeka or moved to the East Coast, but when I think of Beth, I know this is the only place I could be. She is a healer, shaman, medicine woman. I can feel and hear her listening. From the core of her being, she is the definition of a therapist.

Micki is my two-year-old mini-goldendoodle. I never knew I could love anything as much as I love Micki. She is feisty, athletic, and filled with love. Nothing pleases me more than to take her to a dog park. I take off her leash and she dashes around, plays with the other dogs, and expresses complete joy. I love watching her catch up to me. Her head juts forward, back legs fly up, and her ears flap in the wind. In the morning, when I am downstairs and she is asleep on the bed upstairs, I wait for the sound of her paws hitting the steps. It is like Christmas every morning. After I got Micki, I noticed something astounding about her. I was crying and sniffling and trying not to awaken her when she lifted her head up, looked at me, and jumped from the chair to where I was sitting on the couch. She licked my eyes, nose, and face and would not stop until I stopped crying. I always assure her that I am OK. When she feels I am better, she returns to her chair and falls asleep. She is the light of my life and keeps me moving.

www.ingramcontent.com/pod-product-compliance
Lightning Source LLC
LaVergne TN
LVHW041545070426
835507LV00011B/942